COME AS YOU ARE
AFTER EVE KOSOFSKY SEDGWICK

BEFORE YOU START TO READ THIS BOOK, take this moment to think about making a donation to punctum books, an independent non-profit press,

@ https://punctumbooks.com/support/

If you're reading the e-book, you can click on the image below to go directly to our donations site. Any amount, no matter the size, is appreciated and will help us to keep our ship of fools afloat. Contributions from dedicated readers will also help us to keep our commons open and to cultivate new work that can't find a welcoming port elsewhere. Our adventure is not possible without your support.

Vive la Open Access.

Fig. 1. Hieronymus Bosch, *Ship of Fools* (1490–1500)

COME AS YOU ARE. Copyright © 2021 by Jonathan Goldberg. AFTER EVE KOSOFSKY SEDGWICK. Copyright © 1999 by Eve Kosofsky Sedgwick. This work carries a Creative Commons BY-NC-SA 4.0 International license, which means that you are free to copy and redistribute the material in any medium or format, and you may also remix, transform and build upon the material, as long as you clearly attribute the work to the authors (but not in a way that suggests the authors or punctum books endorses you and your work), you do not use this work for commercial gain in any form whatsoever, and that for any remixing and transformation, you distribute your rebuild under the same license. http://creativecommons.org/licenses/by-nc-sa/4.0/

First published in 2021 by dead letter office, BABEL Working Group, an imprint of punctum books, Earth, Milky Way.
https://punctumbooks.com

The BABEL Working Group is a collective and desiring-assemblage of scholar-gypsies with no leaders or followers, no top and no bottom, and only a middle. BABEL roams and stalks the ruins of the post-historical university as a multiplicity, a pack, looking for other roaming packs with which to cohabit and build temporary shelters for intellectual vagabonds. We also take in strays.

ISBN-13: 978-1-953035-43-1 (print)
ISBN-13: 978-1-953035-44-8 (ePDF)

DOI: 10.21983/P3.0342.1.00

LCCN: 2021934829
Library of Congress Cataloging Data is available from the Library of Congress

Copyediting: Lily Brewer
Book design: Vincent W.J. van Gerven Oei
Cover photograph: Eve Kosofsky Sedgwick at SUNY Stony Brook, by H.A. Sedgwick.

HIC SVNT MONSTRA

COME AS YOU ARE

AFTER

EVE KOSOFSKY SEDGWICK

Jonathan Goldberg

*What he has is what you see, and includes the resolve
to get rid of things already absorbed.*

—James Merrill, *Prose of Departure*

Contents

Prefatory · xv

After Eve Kosofsky Sedgwick · 19
   "Then and Now" · 20
   After · 24
   "Reality and Realization" · 26
   "Twisted Temporalities," "Queer Temporality" · 30
   "Eve Sedgwick's 'Other Materials'" · 39
   "Come As You Are" · 48
   "Woven Spaces" · 54
   After (again) · 65
   "A Pedagogy of Love" · 72

Come As You Are · 85
   Come as you Are · 86
   Floating Columns / In the Bardo · 109

Illustrations
   SUNY Stony Brook, Fall 1999 · 112
   CUNY Graduate Center, Spring 2000 · 123

Works Cited · 125

Acknowledgments

I am happy to be published again by punctum books in Eileen Joy's Dead Letter Office series. Once again Vincent W. J. van Gerven Oei has designed a wonderful cover and expertly guided the book through production; I am very grateful to him for his warm attention. Lily Brewer copy edited lightly and admirably.

The photographs in the book were taken by Hal Sedgwick; I thank him for providing them and allowing me to choose some to represent the exhibits of Eve's work that accompanied her delivery of "Come as Your Are." I am grateful for Hal's support and enthusiasm for this project, and hope he will be happy with the results.

Melissa Solomon provided me with some copy texts for which I am grateful, as well as for the memories of Eve she shared with me. Jason Edwards kindly allowed me to see a copy of his forthcoming book on Eve's art work.

In the course of putting this volume together I have relied on Hal Rogers for unfailing support and advice. This project began in the fall 2019 semester when I sat in on a seminar on Eve's work and legacy that Michael Moon conducted; I am grateful to that occasion and the conversations and thoughts it provoked. "After Eve Kosofsky Sedgwick" was prompted by the critics we read; in conversation with them, I turn to Eve's work, its continuing provocations to thought. Michael read every page of this volume, in all its incarnations, always with loving interest and enthusiasm. Eve remarks in *Tendencies* on Michael's extraordinary, infectious capacities for *being interested.* I have been sustained by that — and by his love — for more than thirty-five years. This volume is but the latest instance of what he makes possible.

Prefatory

This book brings together two pieces of writing. In the first, "After Eve Kosofsky Sedgwick," I continue (expand, reiterate) analysis of Eve's work that motivated two earlier essays entitled "On the Eve of the Future" as well as "Eve's Future Figures." They posit a futurity also conveyed by "after": those of us who write after Eve's death see her as before us. In more than one sense we come after her. As Ramzi Fawaz writes in his introduction to *Reading Sedgwick*, Eve's "work was always aspirational and anticipatory." It aims to "confer plenitude on ... the field of critical thought" and offers "*all of us* ... resources" to do so.[1] In "After Eve Kosofsky Sedgwick," I explore a number of recent responses to that call as I attend to how Eve's late work extends the reach of queer theory — its "perverse, desiring energies that alone can move across ontological thresholds," to borrow Eve's description of the ambitions of *The Warm Decembers*.[2]

"Come As You Are" is a talk Eve delivered at SUNY Stony Brook in fall 1999 and at the CUNY Graduate Center in spring 2000. I might have included it in *The Weather in Proust*, opting

---

[1] Ramzi Fawaz, "'An Open Mesh of Possibilities': The Necessity of Eve Sedgwick in Dark Times," in *Reading Sedgwick*, ed. Lauren Berlant (Durham: Duke University Press, 2019), 27.

[2] Eve Kosofsky Sedgwick, *Fat Art, Thin Art* (Durham: Duke University Press, 1994), 157.

there to print a briefer, earlier version of it, "Reality and Realization," and a later lecture, "Making Things, Practicing Emptiness," that draws upon it: I relegated salient passages not found in those pieces to footnotes, and two poems of Eve's quoted in it to my introduction. Scott Herring's "Eve Sedgwick's 'Other Materials'" prompted me to make the entire lecture available. When I first contemplated writing more about Eve's work, I had the feeling that I would want to put my essay beside "Come As You Are," but it was only in writing "After Eve Kosofsky Sedgwick" that I came to understand that feeling; that realization gets worked out in the middle of my essay as I write about Scott's — it offers a reading of "Come As You Are" avant la lettre, as it were, since all Scott had before him were its dispersed pieces in *The Weather in Proust*.

Readers of this book may well want to start with Eve's piece. However familiar some of it may be, it has its own logic, its own organization. Scott's essay provides one way into it. In my essay, I focus on its questions about determination — overdetermination and underdetermination. Determination sounds closer to the former in this pair of supposed opposites except for the fact that "de" can't help but suggest its own negation. Such doubleness, its ontological purchase across boundaries, is my concern. It was a place Eve liked to be, as she told Stephen Barber and David Clark, "I'm always compelled by the place where a project of writing runs into things that I just can't say. ... That's the unrationalizable place that seems worth being to me, often the only place that seems worth being."[3]

In my essay, I refer to Eve as "Eve" more often than not, and have allowed first names in when commenting on the work of others I know (or knew) personally. I do this not to prioritize that mode of relation; in fact, something else is central to my essay. Like Fawaz, who "never 'met' [Eve] except in and through her

---

[3] Stephen M. Barber and David L. Clark, "This Piercing Bouquet: An Interview with Eve Kosofsky Sedgwick," in *Regarding Sedgwick*, eds. Stephen M. Barber and David L. Clark (New York: Routledge, 2002), 246.

textual performances" (27), I see the Eve(s) in her text as most "available" to *all of us*. As Fawaz suggests, her work is both extraordinarily specific and yet generalizable, precise and deeply suggestive. As I will be arguing, it extends likeness that does not preclude difference but rather sustains identity as a site of multiple identifications, as Fawaz also affirms. The Eve anyone knew is only one site of the possibilities her work explores and opens (and to which she opened herself). As she writes at the end of "Queer and Now," her writing "laminates" the possibility of making a "different thing" happen" through "the circuit of contagion, fun, voyeurism, envy, participation, and stimulation" in which occur the multiple, conflicting, processes of (dis)identification that "so many people need."[4]

---

[4] Eve Kososfsky Sedgwick, *Tendencies* (Durham: Duke University Press, 1993), 19–20.

After Eve Kosofsky Sedgwick

Jonathan Goldberg

A year after Eve Sedgwick died, Michael Moon and I taught a graduate seminar on her work; "Reading Sedgwick" surveyed publications from the 1980s to the mid-'90s that came to be categorized as queer theory as well as some of Eve's later work in affect theory, Buddhism, and textiles. Ten years after Eve's death, for his final graduate seminar before retirement, Michael offered a course on her legacy. I attended many of the classes. Its focus was on later work and responses to it in the past ten years. "After Eve Kosofsky Sedgwick" was prompted by that reading. Coincidentally, "Eve's Future Figures," an essay I wrote soon after Eve's death that includes reflections on our 2010 seminar, appeared in *Reading Sedgwick*. Lauren Berlant opens the volume with "Reading Sedgwick, Then and Now." I begin here with her timely reflections. My essay, although occasioned by the brief history I just offered, explores questions that have motivated my work since *The Seeds of Things,* published, "as it happens," a few months after Eve's death, although finished months before she died. Eve has been "behind" my work, at least since *Sodometries*, if not before; and always ahead. No one has mattered more to me in this respect; others, however different from me they are, feel the same way. That relationship also is a topic in what follows.

"Then and Now"

As Lauren Berlant notes, *Reading Sedgwick* was initiated by Michael O'Rourke soon after Eve died on April 12, 2009. As H.A. Sedgwick, Eve's husband, Hal, details in his prefatory note to the collection, half of the essays in the volume originated in papers given at three sessions commemorating Eve at the 2010 Modern Language Association convention. The divide between those writing "then" and the ones written "now," joined in Berlant's collection and acknowledged in the title of her preface, is complicated from its opening sentence on: "This book calls up multiple pasts that are not past."[1] "Then," in this formulation, remains "now," as it still is when the preface concludes by characterizing "now" as an "iteration of the reactionary turn" of the "then," the time when Eve first intervened: that reiteration "makes the Eve who diagnosed the 'then' even more newly necessary in the emerging and solidifying 'now'" (4). These uses of "now" and "then" recall in advance the subtitle of Fawaz's introduction, "The Necessity of Eve Sedgwick in Dark Times." "Now" and "then," destabilized by scare quotes, join in a reiteration that remains bound to dark times.

Nonetheless, it can seem as if the writing of the Eve who passed remains in the past, especially when it is described as "occasional" and "situational." Likewise, the essays written now seem timebound when they are said to show "the presence of their situatedness" through their "reenactment ... in or around Eve" (1). Parsing the temporal relation between the situational and the reiterated is difficult, although tilted in one direction when Eve's formative queer theory is located in the Reagan years, while her later work in reparation, affect theory, and "Buddhist metempsychoses" (4) is dated to the heady, delusional Obama era. (In fact, most of Eve's work dates from the Bush and Clinton years.) "Now" and "Then" offer "situational writing from specific historical moments" (1). "Those of us for whom

---

1   Lauren Berlant, "Reading Sedgwick, Then and Now," in *Reading Sedgwick*, ed. Lauren Berlant (Durham: Duke University Press, 2019), 1.

Eve was a living presence at very specific historic conjunctures" are divided from the current "generation of scholars who can assume queerness." (2). For "us who were Eve's contemporaries, the questions are different": how to continue our attachment to her is one; "how do we continue the project of coming to terms with what we can't specifically have asked for" (2) another.

These questions of continuity question the limits of the specificity of a life — of a then and now — beside something that survives, persists, desired and yet unexpected; that something, I would venture, also may define a life — a then or a now — and, so doing, put pressure on those temporal markers the way Berlant does at the beginning and end of her preface. What persists is further remarked when she invokes the multiple "modes" of Eve's "being herself for her friends, students, colleagues, and for criticism" (1). The last of these involves her many styles of writing. If the essays gathered in *Reading Sedgwick* share "a strong mimetic drive to be with Eve by being like Eve" (1–2), that likeness cannot be reduced to a singularity. And when the essays are further described as resulting from "individual decisions about retaining and erasing traces of their origins" (1), retention and erasure arguably surpass individual decisions. The persistence of reiteration across now and then also points this way, prompting the reiterative, retrospective effect of the volume that Berlant aptly terms "queer respect" (1).

How definitive is the distinction between those whose relation to Eve is "an attachment known only through her writing" from those of "us for whom Eve was a living presence" (2)? I certainly belong in that latter group: Eve and I were friends for the last twenty years of her life, from soon after she joined the Duke English Department, when Michael Moon, who had taken a position there a year or two before, moved into her house. I lived with them on Montgomery Street weekends, summers, on sabbaticals. I went with Eve to her doctor when she got her initial cancer diagnosis; I cooked dinner for her during her subsequent round of chemo. With Michael and Hal, I sat at her bedside during her last days. She entrusted her late writing to me to edit and publish.

Certainly, I knew and loved and admired Eve. Lauren asks, for those of us who knew her, "what it meant, and still means to be writing with Eve not just on, but in, our minds" (2). It makes a difference but not a categorical one since, as she also says, the modes of writing in which Eve offered herself through the powerful heuristic of the "I" inscribes a position any of us can variously inhabit. To put this another way, I would recall what I wrote in "On the Eve of the Future," and quote in "Eve's Future Figures," about what Eve meant by the reality that survives one's own death or the painful loss of someone deeply loved: "Eve herself was irreplaceable, but also not singular. As she insists in "The Weather in Proust," one meaning of supra-individuality is that one is connected and constituted beyond oneself, connected thereby to versions of oneself that succeed oneself ... the life beyond life that inheres in relation that exceeds and constitutes the individual."[2] Writing, one of the places where that life continues to exist, continues beyond our own lives.

*

In the pages that follow I revisit Eve in the spirit that Philomina Tsoukala affirms. Writing about the visceral effect of reading a writer known only through her writing, Tsoukala found that Eve "seemed to be ages ahead of me."[3] This is not a chronological reckoning: Eve knows her better than Tsoukala knows herself. This allows her, in writing, to be where Eve is, indeed to be vicariously, physically, sexually, psychologically, with her. Many readers have had versions of this feeling on first reading Eve. Lauren attests to it in "Two Girls, Fat and Thin" when she records her initial excitement on encountering Eve's writing, its espousal of attachments capable of "unsurpassable consequence," "an attitude toward what thinking (as *écriture*) can do";

---

[2] Jonathan Goldberg, "On the Eve of the Future," *PMLA* 125, no. 2 (March 2010): 376.

[3] Philomina Tsoukala, "Reading 'A Poem is Being Written,'" *Harvard Journal of Law & Gender* 33, no. 1 (Winter 2010): 343.

"Attachments are made … by an intelligence after which we are always running."[4] In following after Eve, she is at once past and yet before us. We come running after.

*

Although I knew Eve well for many years, in person and on the page, my first actual meeting with her, at English Institute in 1984 I believe, was not very auspicious. *Between Men* was forthcoming, and I wanted to talk about it. Eve wanted only to talk about getting back to *The Warm Decembers*. We got nowhere. I read *Between Men* and published a review of the chapter on Shakespeare's sonnets, alongside some other work on sexuality in the early modern period, in GSN, the gay studies newsletter edited by Michael Lynch that was the forerunner of GLQ. While I appreciated Eve's forthright acknowledgment of male-male erotics — and female sexuality, too, in Shakespeare's sonnets — I worried about her recourse to "heterosexuality" as the only term to describe sexuality in a culture that didn't have "homosexuality" in its lexicon. A few years ago, at a conference occasioned by the thirtieth anniversary of the publication of *Between Men*, I gave a paper entitled "Misgivings" in which I rehearsed my early response. I did it in part to make reparations (I came to see how powerful Eve's argument was and that I had misread it initially), but mostly because it suggested something more important: Eve's writing is powerfully present precisely because it is always ahead of us; ahead of her too. Having Eve in mind does not happen in the same way to all of us, or in the same way for any one of us whenever we encounter her texts. Lauren knows this too. Soon after Eve's death, in "Eve Sedgwick, Once More," she describes her first encounter with Eve's writing this way: "it had made me gasp, resist, have reveries, think twice, think

---

4 Lauren Berlant, "Two Girls, Fat and Thin," in *Regarding Sedgwick: Essays on Queer Culture and Critical Theory*, eds. Stephen M. Barber and David L. Clark (New York: Routledge, 2002), 71, 73, 74.

bigger, and become different."[5] Judith Butler reports something akin in "Capacity," about reading and rereading *Between Men*: "each time I was being asked to think differently than I usually do."[6] Eve is always before us, the locus of misgivings that may be missed opportunities to think again or may afford us — whoever we are at whatever moment of reading — possibilities we didn't know we could grasp. They resonate beyond the present, but still in a present that will inevitably not include us as one kind of "living presence." Such an absence does not deny, as Berlant intimates, how she still lives.

After

In "Bringing Out D.A. Miller," on Miller's stance in *Bringing Out Roland Barthes,* Barbara Johnson distinguishes between "outing" and "bringing out." Questions of temporality are involved. In each of its instances, outing means to be a once-for-all affair marked by before/after parameters, a decisive conversion. "Bringing out," whose stylistic import Johnson stresses, entails revelations that are partial, piecemeal, matters of emphasis or occlusion — what is shown, brought out, necessarily leaves other things in the shadows, unsaid, concealed from view. Revelation is a process; it requires time to take place; it does not necessarily end. Johnson connects it to the Delphic command "know thyself." That too is not a once-for-all event. "The Delphic oracle doesn't ask, doesn't tell, and doesn't pursue," she wittily comments, drawing on the language around gays in the US military that leaves unsaid what remains to be (un)said.[7]

"Bringing out" always comes after. Might that temporality reflect "the body's own denial of the category of identity" (7),

---

[5] Lauren Berlant, "Eve Sedgwick, Once More," *Critical Inquiry* 35, no. 4 (Summer 2009): 1089.

[6] Judith Butler, "Capacity," in *Regarding Sedgwick: Essays on Queer Culture and Critical Theory,* eds. Stephen M. Barber and David L. Clark (New York: Routledge, 2002), 109.

[7] Barbara Johnson, "Bringing Out D.A. Miller," *Narrative* 10, no. 1 (January 2002): 5.

Johnson wonders (perhaps in the vein of Maurice Merleau-Ponty in "Indirect Language and the Voices of Silence"). What if the before and after of outing were not the story line that accompanies identity? Or, to ask the question differently, what if that story was tied to a real that co-exists with and yet lies to the side of the reality conferred and designated by distinctions such as those that link "before" to "after"? To ask this is to glimpse — to posit — a reality that is both before and after. That is the temporal framework in which I would situate — bring out — axiom one in *Epistemology of the Closet*: *"People are different from each other."*[8] Its bottom line of singularity is announced through the word "different." Difference is not an identity. Indeed, it is close to its opposite (although it might not be non-identity either). Axiom one might well restate the injunction enjoined by the Delphic Oracle. It is, at any rate, an oracular utterance. "Different" could be the adjective to describe the verbal force that Johnson explores as "bringing out," an utterance whose imperative — to act — is at the same time recursive. It intimates a turning rather than a definitive movement from one thing or state to another, from one time to another. These questions about identity — outed or brought out, lead Johnson, Miller, and me as well, to ask how an author is in her text. Johnson answers by noting that "it is impossible to know whether one is bringing out the person or the writings. And *that* is what Barthes means by 'the death of the author'" (8).

*

Johnson's essay is not about Sedgwick. Nonetheless her parsing of Miller's "bringing out" seems to me suggestive for reading Eve. Writing about the opening sentence of *Bringing Out Roland Barthes* Johnson notices how Miller makes "us believe in the reality of the voice of the living person" (8). Eve does that particularly stunningly at the close of "White Glasses," a eulogy for

---

8   Eve Kosofsky Sedgwick, *Epistemology of the Closet* (Berkeley: University of California Press, 1990), 22.

Michael Lynch that Eve was able to deliver while he still lived. Exploring their identifications, the essay involves the crossing of life and death: Eve's unanticipated cancer diagnosis brings with it another suspended death sentence. Writing takes place in this suspension, the uncanny temporality of the after, the time that remains.

*

> Hi Michael! I know I probably got almost everything wrong but I hope you didn't just hate this. See you in a couple of weeks. (*Tendencies*, 266)

"Reality and Realization"

First published in *The Weather in Proust*, "Reality and Realization" was delivered at the 1998 convention of the Modern Language Association. Eve opens by glancing at her ambition to explore the conjunction she calls "Critical Theory, Buddhist Practice," seemingly as an academic project — an anthology or a conference are mentioned as two possible forms it might take. It could be that, but Eve's gloss on the topic by way of its foundation in "shared nondualistic understandings of more or other than a series of propositional readings" suggests something else, something "more or other," a "sharing" of what they have in common that the terms "Critical" and "Buddhist" do not themselves convey since they do not align along any axis of definitional similarity ("Theory" and "Practice" usually are treated as opposites).[9] Possibilities are furthered when Eve pluralizes "understandings" of "Theory," as "deconstruction or, say, systems theory" (207). She illuminates the nondualism of these gestures later in the essay when she quotes Dudjom Rinpoche's description of the nature of mind: "It has never been liberated /

---

9 Eve Kosofsky Sedgwick, *The Weather in Proust* (Durham: Duke University Press, 2011), 207.

It has never been deluded / It has never existed / It has never been nonexistent" (209).

Like Barbara Johnson's "bringing out" project, Eve's seeks to supplement propositional thinking that aims at the definitive — at identity — with a capacity of identification in which "more" or "other" are not incompatible (they are coupled with an "or" that could as easily be an "and"). The form of knowing that they support is "more an issue of practice ... than of epistemology" (207), less something to know than a way of knowing, doing, and being.

Conceptual and historical parameters of Eve's academic project are sketched in the second paragraph of "Reality and Realization," which glances at moments when Buddhism and western thought came together in a number of thinkers, unnamed, who might "reflect a zeitgeist or two (or twenty)" (206). "Stories that await telling" remain untold, however, except in gestures to names of places and groups. (Fuller consideration of these topics is given in "Pedagogy of Buddhism" in *Touching Feeling*.) The paragraph that follows moves on to "another set of stories," those that ally theory and Buddhism. But rather than pursue these agendas, or to do so otherwise, in lieu of them, Eve offers "a slight but true story" (207) about her own preparation for foreign travel and her experiences in Asia. She reads guidebooks to know what to expect and how to behave. This travel is literal, yet it bears upon her project and its reach; Eve had called the conjunction of theory and practice, criticism and Buddhism "*haimish* to anyone whose mother's milk has been deconstruction or, say, systems theory" (207). In these conjunctions, the at-home and the exotic come together, embodied in a digestive process.

The "slight" story on offer bears the weight of demonstrating "the troubled mismatch between knowledge and realization" that constitutes one of "the distinctive bonds" that tie together "the shared nondualistic understandings" of critical theory and Buddhist thought (207). It hinges on the ubiquity of gift exchange in Asia. Eve couches the lesson taught in all the guidebooks as a maternal dictum: "Remember? We talked about this at home. Now, when you hand over this present, what do you do?" (208) The answer is, you use both hands. As Eve tells the story, it appears that is exactly what she forgot to do, or forgot the dictum in doing. Knowing and realizing meet there. And why not? The story is about exchange, this for that, this or that, making equivalent the non-equivalent, something suggested as well by the variousness of the gifts Eve bears, theory books, maple syrup, baby gifts. Eve's destination is at once *heimlich* and *unheimlich*; to Asia, but to her brother's home and his newborn son (the baby's mother Songmin is named, but not identified as David Kosofsky's wife). The story seems to show that Eve failed to realize what she knew — use two hands — but that an exchange was nonetheless accomplished, took place even if the propositional injunction was not followed or not kept in mind. Realization has "nothing necessarily transcendent about" it after all (209); it lies in the doing. Exchange, anthropologists like Claude Lévi-Strauss and Marcel Mauss before him taught us, is the basis of culture: women, goods, words, are their medium. They accomplish their work through transportation, transposition, displacement and alienation. While there is nothing necessarily transcendent in these material movements, the doing involves the displacement inherent in tying the concept of the gift, definitionally a giving without exchange, to a relationship of exchange, singlehandedness to two-handedness, identity to identification.

The title "Reality and Realization" couples two terms that could appear to name the same thing twice or to name two things that seem almost impossible to distinguish and which nonetheless are as distinct as the two words are. What these words share, Eve claims, is an "orthogonal" relationship to propositional truth (208) — the numerous true statements one might make about any situation will never coincide with the reality of any moment. The temporality of that moment is not easily described. Realization lags behind knowledge "by months or eons" (209), a timespan akin to the zeitgeist or two or twenty of east-west encounters. In the gap between propositional knowledge and its realization, practice endlessly recurs. Eve illuminates it through the concept of the bardo, an in-between state in which one is suspended, in dreams, in meditation, in death. The latter is a privileged state called the bardo of Dharmata, the bardo of reality. It begins immediately after death. Any bardo is meant to open the eyes of practitioners to the realization that any moment is one of in-between suspension. For Eve, that realization came around death, as it did for Johnson by way of Roland Barthes on the death of the author. It was "learning that a cancer I had thought was in remission had in fact become incurable" that brought home "the considerable distance between *knowing* that one will die and *realizing* it" (210). To which one must add, as Eve does, the fact that such a realization is "coupled with the seemingly absolute inaccessibility of our own death to our living consciousness" (210). The coupling of reality and realization occurs in a suspension and gap that never is overcome until it is realized in a place or time inaccessible to "living consciousness": this is where our (mortal) being coincides with Being, with what is. As Sedgwick repeatedly suggests, this is where theory, with its propositional truth claims, lags behind Buddhist practices.

Beside any cause-effect, before-after propositional logic, such practices follow the maternal injunction that one is bound to remember to forget. Never achieving the goal of mastery, the finality of knowing, these practices of mindfulness take place in a now that is a between or a beside. Their "real, obscure temporality" (210) is an after that looks ahead at what is before, ontologically an *unheimlich* heimat, an "itself" that also is "ourselves and not other than ourselves" (211).

*

"I know I probably got almost everything wrong," Eve says to Michael Lynch, that is to say, I know what the Delphic oracle was urging on me, a practice of knowing coincident with not knowing. So "I" can be wrong about almost everything but not about the possibility that Eve's "I" assays when she sends her greeting across what propositional thinking supposes to be the uncrossable boundary between life and death.

"Twisted Temporalities," "Queer Temporality"

These two phrases appear in the titles of two versions of Jane Gallop's 2011 essay on Eve, "Sedgwick's Twisted Temporalities," from which I will be quoting, and "The Queer Temporality of Writing," in which she extends her reading of Eve to the other authors she considers in *The Deaths of the Author*. Gallop fetches the latter phrase from Barber and Clark's introduction to *Regarding Sedgwick*. The "queer temporality" she has in mind, as she notes there, and again in "Early and Earlier Sedgwick," her contribution to *Reading Sedgwick*, is borrowed from Barber and Clark. In that later piece, she takes stock of Eve's authorial revisitations in prefaces to the 1992 reissue of *Between Men* and the republication of *The Coherence of Gothic Fiction* in 1986. Gallop registers shock at the self-divisions that Eve performs in these pieces of writing, the author doubled by death and desire, split between first and third persons. Eve's return to earlier Eves frames Gallop's review of her own earlier essay, my focus here. In that piece, "White Glasses," along with Eve's "Memorial for Craig Owens," are read closely. Both appear in *Tendencies*, and her readings grapple to define the queer moment that volume announces.

To do that, Gallop embraces Barber and Clark's claim that a "specifically queer temporality" in *Tendencies* jostles "a recognizable temporal frame, ... another conception and unfolding of temporality" (2). In a footnote at the end of her essay, she offers a gloss by quoting "White Glasses," where Eve writes, "what is at work here ... falls ... across the ontological crack between the living and the dead."[10] That between could be teased perhaps from the title of the first essay in *Tendencies*, "Queer and Now." It couples "queer" to a temporal marker by way of the little word "and" (to recall Wagner's Isolde on the "und" that joins her to Tristan). "Something about *queer* is inextinguishable" is Eve's

---

10 Jane Gallop, "Sedgwick's Twisted Temporalities," in *Queer Times, Queer Becomings*, eds. E.L. McCallum and Mikko Tukhanen (Albany: SUNY Press, 2011), 73n25.

numinous gloss on the "now" of queer (*Tendencies* xii), as she traces the etymological roots of the word, "twist" among them. Gallop chooses that word to focus queer temporality in relation to the writing that survives the death of the author. Eve emphasizes its transitivity, its mobile motion across.

The queer twist on temporality in Gallop's essay becomes an ironic twist: "the slow organic temporality" (57) of expectation suffers the sudden surprise of its bafflement by death. The end of life ends the writing process; before and after are in a relation of estrangement and distortion. These ironic twists are directed against the writer's attempt at mastery of the situation. The writer is both Eve and Jane Gallop herself: at the very moment Gallop finds Sedgwick having trouble writing she adds a footnote to confess her own difficulty finishing her essay. Both writers overcome their difficulty, however, Eve in the completed essay, "Tales of the Avunculate," which takes up a prompt from Craig Owens, as well as in the uncanny liveness of her address to Michael Lynch in "White Glasses." Picking up on Eve's claim in the foreword to *Tendencies* that "queer" is a "continuing moment," Gallop links the present tense utterance of Eve to Michael Lynch as one that stands outside temporality in its refusal of the rhythm of expectation and fulfilment whose disruptions her readings chart. By staying behind, it becomes anachronistic. Lynch gets to hear his obituary; he is "still alive and already dead," she writes, "a very unsettling moment .... out of and in time" (70). In a final ironic twist, the framework of before and after interrupted by the unbridgeable gap between life and death is joined in an "and."

It always is "and" in Sedgwick's writing. Gallop's gap — and the "or" it supposes — is only part of the story. Following Barber and Clark who find the celebration of queer at the opening of *Tendencies* "hedged," Gallop locates Eve's hesitation to celebrate the visible arrival of the queer moment as the temporal distortion AIDS introduced into the queer parade, at once a slowing down of life to good days and bad ones, and a speeding up to a precipitous end. Gallop extends this distortion to the grammar of Eve's sentence, relocating a parenthesis she thinks starts in the wrong place and includes issues that don't belong together. "The long parenthesis distorts the text. AIDS and death are part of that distortion," she writes (52). The issues in the parenthesis are indeed far from univocal; they include signs of gay acceptance — by the incoming president (Clinton), in the strong presence of people of color for the first time in the annual gay march; of stigma and prejudice against people with AIDS; of misguided straight and gay politics — the embrace of bisexuality and of military service. That is their point: all these "other moments" than the queer moment nonetheless coincide in it. Queer time is a matter of either/or and of both/and.

Gallop worries the temporal relationship of *Tendencies* and *Epistemology of the Closet,* emphasizing the distance between them, claiming that Eve's stress on their proximity "would minimize almost out of existence" (48) the three years that separate the two books. Death marks this difference. Similarly, she emphasizes how the death of Craig Owens robbed Eve of any motive to finish writing her essay. "Suddenly I couldn't do that," Eve writes (105–6); "Sedgwick is having a hard time writing," "Sedgwick underscores how difficult writing was," "Sedgwick is having a very hard time writing," she reiterates (57). "As it turns out, however, the memorial's sense of impossibility is in fact only temporary," Gallop admits a couple of pages later (59), going on to glance at "Tales of the Avunculate," which she first summarizes accurately enough as involving "the queer in the family," but then, just as quickly, moves to its ironic twist, declaring the conclusion of that essay a surprise and abruption in its "militant rejection of the family" (60).

This moment of surprise could be put beside an earlier one that Gallop notices when she compares "a feature of queer possibility" that Eve explores in Proust (in "Paranoid and Reparative Reading") to the foreshortening of AIDS: "first she establishes deroutinized temporality as an attractive, even joyful possession, before she links it to brutality and death," she writes (51). The two are not quite so disjunct; the "temporal disorientation," Sedgwick writes, of this "revelatory space would have been impossible in a heterosexual *père de famille,* in one who had meanwhile been embodying, in the form of inexorably 'progressing' identities and roles, the regular arrival of children and grandchildren."[11] The assault on the family, its opacity about the queer in the family, points to the "something" in queer that remains inextinguishable: a revelatory space of realization of survival despite the power of ignorance, denial, exclusion, and stigma. Its coincidence of temporalities is akin to the coincidence of minoritizing and universalizing impulses in the formation of sexual identities that enable "relational and strange" movements across boundaries, even including the ontological divide of life and death.

For another boundary crossed in Eve, consider Gallop's excision of Audre Lorde's name from her citation and close reading of the parenthesis at the opening of *Tendencies* (52) in which Eve names together the AIDS deaths of Tom Yingling and Melvin Dixon and Lorde's from cancer. In footnote 20, close to the end of "Twisted Temporalities," Gallop acknowledges her omission, claiming that her heightening of the ironic twist follows Eve since she does not immediately reveal her cancer diagnosis in "White Glasses." AIDS and cancer, however, are coincident from the start of *Tendencies,* part of Eve's pursuit of sameness and difference across gender and race, among other categories.

Although the death of the author and the liveness of writing are her ultimate concerns, Gallop's essay on Eve's temporalities narrows its focus to writing in its most literal sense. Her analysis of the "Memorial for Craig Owens" follows from Eve's first meeting him in print (in an essay in which he singled her out from other feminists for her anti-homophobic argument connecting women and gay men) to his death while Eve was writing "Tales of the Avunculate." "Relation" is a key term in the memorial. It involves "part-objects," writing serving as a main example of the materials of a strange and strangely familiar relationship.

---

11 Eve Kosofsky Sedgwick, "Paranoid Reading and Reparative Reading; or, You're So Paranoid, You Probably Think This Introduction Is About You," in *Novel Gazing: Queer Readings in Fiction* (Durham: Duke University Press, 1997), 26.

Gallop attaches to it a Freudian frame of perversity. That might be part of the story; Eve's invocation of the term certainly is indebted to Melanie Klein and D.W. Winnicott's development of object relations. Eve's "motive," she writes in the memorial, goes "very deep" and seems immemorial (104). Begun in writing, it continued when she and Craig Owens met: "seeing him felt like keeping an assignation we'd always had, and it felt that way to me each of the few times we got to see each other" (104). "Always" disrupts the sequence.

What continues is not something easily parsed. Eve makes no claim to know what Craig Owens really was "like," whether her relation to him was one that others who knew him would have recognized, or whether he would have articulated their relation in the same way. Not knowing such things, a point she emphasizes, does not preclude knowing that somehow what they exchanged was something that neither of them "had a right to be surprised" by (104). So, to the surprise of the interruption of death add a matching non-surprise of a non-equivalent equivalence between things and persons unlike yet like each other. From the elements of his "differential social identity," Owens offered Eve a place for her "identificatory life" answered by the "parts" of her that "might be ... inside Craig" (105), "a durable motive that went very deep" in both directions. "I can't imagine yet what will happen to the motive Craig provided in me," she writes; "Craig's vitality" is that motive, the motor force that he "animated with both his presences and absences," "this strange, utterly discontinuous, projective space of desire euphemistically named friendship, love at a distance, or even just reading and writing" (105). Crucial to this discontinuity and difference is precisely its power to continue beyond the person even as it contributes to "all the different surfaces that make a self for most of us" (104).

This conjunction defines "what falling in love means" to Eve, she writes in *A Dialogue on Love*: "It's a matter of suddenly, globally, 'knowing' that another person represents your only access to some vitally,

transmissible truth
or radiantly heightened
mode of perception,

and that if you lose the thread of intimacy, both you and your whole world might subsist forever in some desert-like state of ontological impoverishment."[12] "Knowing" is in scare quotes here because what Eve describes is a realization that is self-constitutive yet made in relation to another, or to an otherness in the beloved whose vitality, whose life, shared, provides the access point for truths and perceptions that are likewise transpersonal and impersonal, intimate and radiant. The ontological richness of this relationship cannot be divorced from its being merely a thread in some weaving that is not one's own and yet constitutes one's self in a world.

In formulations like these, object relations inhere not only *as* objects, but *in* objects, including the ones we are in relation to what is strange, not us and yet us. It might be found in "a couple of cryptic paragraphs" we try to decipher (*Tendencies* 105). "The verbal aura that attached to this cherished adhesion," Eve writes, using Whitman's preferred term for relation, "hovered around the magical words, enigmatic, magnetic" (106). She worries at the end of her obituary that what will now "unfold and unfold" in her will be the loss of this cherished "subject and object." Although she genuinely does not know what will come of loss, what happens is inherent in strange relations that exceed what an "I" might know, a knowledge not entirely one's own to know even as it inhabits one's writing and being, a relationship to others and past them too: "Now the sense of gratitude and luck, which painfully can't diminish, are fermenting around I can't tell what point of adhesion — since I feel I genuinely don't know if this inexorable disclosure now can unfold anything but, repeatedly, the loss of its subject and object" (106). The gratitude, and the motive it carries are equally inexorable: On the one hand,

---

[12] Eve Kosofsky Sedgwick, *A Dialogue on Love* (Boston: Beacon Press, 1999), 168.

nothing lasts forever; on the other, something goes on. Writing is one name for that something inextinguishable. "The eventual unfolding of that enclosure, already internal, was part of what, I always thought, was going to constitute me: for better and maybe also worse, for comfort and conceivably danger" (106).

The memorial thus ends with something still fermenting. So, too, the uncanny voice at the end of "White Glasses" persists beyond the bounds of life and death. Gallop acknowledges this glancing at the dedication page of *Tendencies*, three photos of Eve and Michael at the grave of Emily Dickinson, and the words, "In memory of Michael Lynch, and with love to him." "I thought I would have to — I thought I could — address this to you instead of Michael," Eve addresses the audience of presumed mourners, "and now (yikes) I can do both" (256). In the dedication she does both too, sending her love to dead Michael Lynch. This queer motion (motive) athwart moves across the divide: "Now, shock and mourning gaze in both directions through the obituary frame, and much more than shock and mourning, it is exciting that Michael is alive and full of beans today, sick as he is; I think it is exciting for both of us that I am; and in many ways it is full of stimulation and interest, even, to be ill and writing" (256).

"The I who does both is also a different one with new fears and temporalities" (256). The name for that new time at the conclusion of "White Glasses" is "this long moment," and Eve longs "to know more and more" about it (266). The way through and across it is captured in a line from the poem by Ariwara no Narihara that Eve stenciled on to her fabric art: "I have always known that I would take this path, but yesterday I did not know it would be today" (*Weather in Proust* 111). Commenting on it, Eve remarks her fondness for weaving herself into an "I" that is not herself, one, moreover, on the point of unraveling. That point is the nexus of her identifications across, for her "real dread" is not of dying before her time, "but about losing the people who make ... [her] want to live" (*Tendencies* 264). In the obituary relation, "anyone, living or dead, may occupy the position of the speaker, the spoken to, the spoken about" (264). These crossings at "the ontological crack between the living and the dead" move along the axis of "an identification that falls across gender ... sexualities ... 'perversions'" (257).

If so-called "organic" temporality supposes that one thing follows another, it's worth noticing how, in "White Glasses," that's not how the writing proceeds, and not just in the volte-faces on which Gallop fastens. Eve begins with her first meeting with Michael Lynch three times in topic sentences that vary slightly, same and different at once: "The first time I met Michael Lynch ...," "When I first met Michael Lynch ...," "The day I first met Michael Lynch" (252–53). These are, perhaps, tellings of the same encounter, involving the same persons, the "I" and "Michael Lynch"; Eve first focuses on his white glasses, her belief that within a year every gay man will be sporting them; she resolves: "I want to be first." She wants to be first, before all the other gay men, but after Michael Lynch. The object that would retrospectively put her in his position is precisely that, an object. White glasses matter here as a prosthetic non-organic extension that prolongs relation beyond any recognizable likeness to make them "like."

The second "first" situates Michael differently, not through his glasses but in terms of his contributions to gay studies and gay activism, a part he plays and to which he attracts and attaches others. It places him in a then tiny field of academia: everyone who fits the bill gathers in a coffee shop at the 1986 MLA convention. Finally, another "first": Michael Lynch's ex, Bill Lewis, has just been diagnosed with AIDS: "the Michael I met and fell in love with, was to some degree I could never estimate, a Michael made different on the same day by the suddenly more graphic proximity of intimate loss" (253). Its effect? It enhanced "Michael's availability to be identified with and loved." By becoming other than himself, Michael has begun to know and to arrive at that boundary to which Eve was drawn in an identification that began in an object (white glasses). It issues immediately in this statement of identity/identification: "the I who met Michael and fell in love with his white glasses ... was nobody simpler than the handsome and complicated poet and scholar I met in him" (253).

For an image to accompany this, I, like Jane Gallop, turn to the dedication page of *Tendencies,* the photo collage of Eve and Michael at the tomb of Emily Dickinson that Jason Edwards informs us was titled "Eternity's White Flag." "Sedgwick and Lynch tenderly interlocked over Dickinson's grave," Jason writes.[13] Eve's identification as a gay man passed through her and Michael's differentially shared lesbian identification with Dickinson (and with Willa Cather), and through the blanket from the lesbian aunt who raised him that Michael gave Eve after her cancer diagnosis. These fostered a likeness that had nothing to do with how they looked or how white glasses looked on them (Eve provides an exacting discussion of the whiteness of the white glasses in relation to race and gender), nor even how they saw through the funereal frame. White is attached to death and blankness, to the "nobody" simpler and more complicated than one finds in a "fiercely transitive" relation "that might cross barriers" (*Tendencies* 253). Hence Eve's attachment to "the unbearably double-edged imperative" of the reiterated "Out, out" (261):

> She should have died hereafter:
> There would have been a time for such a word, —
> To-morrow, and to-morrow, and to-morrow,
> Creeps in this petty pace from day to day,
> To the last syllable of recorded time;
> And all our yesterdays have lighted fools
> The way to dusty death. Out, out, brief candle!
> Life's but a walking shadow; a poor player,
> That struts and frets his hour upon the stage,
> And then is heard no more: it is a tale
> Told by an idiot, full of sound and fury,
> Signifying nothing.
>
> (*Macbeth* 5.5.17–28)

---

[13] Jason Edwards, *Bathroom Songs: Eve Kosofsky Sedgwick as a Poet* (Earth: punctum books, 2017), 73–74.

Eve reads the inevitable snuffing of the flame of individual life that is ours alongside the "performative injunction" of coming-out, bringing out, being out, "the imperative of visibility, defiance, solidarity, and self-assertion" (261). These are so little opposites that "Out, out" could as soon mean "Include, include." Michael's "availability to identification" is something that Eve claims for herself: "It's as though there were transformative political work to be done just by being available to be identified with in the very grain of one's illness (which is to say, the grain of one's own intellectual, emotional, bodily self as refracted through illness and as resistant to it) — being available for identification to friends, but as well to people who don't love one; even to people who may not like one at all nor wish one well" (261). "I have never felt less stability in my gender, age, and racial identities, nor, anxious and full of the shards of dread, shame, and mourning as this process is, have I ever felt more of a mind to explore and exploit every possibility" (264).The adventure of life/death is not other than the dream of *"dolce far niente"* she hopes for when Michael visits (259), doing and being nothing and nobody, signifying nothing.

"Eve Sedgwick's 'Other Materials'"

My heading is the title of an essay by Scott Herring that has galvanized this book project; more immediately, it furthers my consideration of materiality in Eve's thought. Herring borrows from a course title of Eve's, "How To Do Things with Words and Other Materials." Obliquely, but finally, and centrally, his essay embraces the conjunction of words with other materials that Eve declared a foregone conclusion in her own late fabric art (*Weather in Proust* 106). Most of his essay richly mines Eve's writing, early and late, for material conjunctions, as, for example, in a passage he quotes from *Dialogue of Love*: "THE BUDDHIST STUFF, MANIA FOR MAKING UNSPEAKING OBJECTS" (*Dialogue* 107). As "stuff," Buddhist thought provides a material correlate for the "unspeaking objects" Eve made. In them, her own personhood and agency faced limits she felt in the push back of her materials, inorganic matter with a mind of its own, so to speak, objects insisting on being. Anal matter, Herring argues, is a prime referent for the "other materials" that thread their way through Eve's oeuvre. Following it, he also is led to speculate provocatively on Kleinian object relations. Human psychology moves in the direction of the objects humans produce that are "other" than themselves, evacuated from them. The doubleness of our self/not-our-self marks our existence as not entirely our own. This route leads him to a close consideration of Eve's "Bathroom Song," a poem that moves from her fecal matter to Buddhist stuff.

Herring's essay is supported by the connection Eve makes in "Come As You Are," between letting go of the fecal matter that our bodies produce and the letting go of our bodily life that death entails. Letting be is not only an answer to the unwelcome imperative of death but also a fact of life; we lose "our shit, our eyelashes, our hair, our scabs, our skin, our youth, our hips, our capacities to reproduce, our minds, our lovers, our parents, our bodies, our selves," Herring details.[14] "There is nothing shittier than losing something or someone you love," he continues; his sentence applies as much to our self-relations as it does to our relation to beloved others. Toilet training is the beginning of a lesson in letting go that we come to realize in the death we carry with us. This is a recognition, in Buddhist terms, of the transitoriness of our lives and selves built on a crumbling, unraveling basis of supposed needs and self-aggrandizing desires. "Suppose that getting toilet trained is about learning, forcibly, to change the process of one's person into a residual product — into something that instead exemplifies the impersonal in its lumpishly ultimate taboo form," Eve hypothesizes. "Isn't this one of the tasks of dying as well?" "The silk and the shit again go together," Herring remarks, citing their conjunction in Eve's therapist, Shannon Van Wey's notes that connect Eve's fabric arts to the

---

14 Scott Herring, "Eve Sedgwick's 'Other Materials,'" *Angelaki* 23, no. 1 (February 2018): 14–15.

letting go of self that toilet training initiates (*Dialogue* 206).[15] Letting go is a creative act; it releases a masterpiece, a gift. On earlier pages of *Dialogue on Love,* Eve tells Van Wey about being toilet trained at an improbably early age. In his notes, he speculates, or perhaps voices Eve's speculations about this memory, perhaps a shared family fantasy, in which pride in accomplishment meets shame; it fueled her masturbatory practice and accompanying sexual fantasies of spanking. "HAVING BOTTOM EXPOSED" is what they share (190). What's mused in this material is the punch line in "A Poem Is Being Written," where spanking sparks poetic practice and Eve's creative imagination. Its final metamorphosis was the conjunction of Buddhism, Proust, and textiles — arts of letting go.

Herring connects Eve's late ruminations to her earlier work, her focus on anality in Henry James, for example, or the potty humor of "Divinity," an essay/performance piece Eve co-authored with Michael Moon. In it the cross-gender identification enacted through the cross-dressed fat body of John Waters's star Divine leads to the scene in *Pink Flamingos* in which she eats shit, a symbolic gesture that defines her abjected shameful existence. A Buddhist perspective could rewrite this scenario to underline the possibility of an impersonal place of belonging that has let go of self. This is also a subject in "A Poem Is Being Written." There, the aorist agency of the Freudian scene of the child being beaten entails the de-agential agency of the anal erotics of poetic production.

Herring's analysis traces a path from the erotic emphasis in Eve's earlier work to her later stress on nondualism, a way of putting one thing beside another, life and death in relation by way of the sexuality inherent in the non-sexual reproduction of anal sex. The paradigmatic instance of this creative conjunction is a passage in Henry James's notebook that Eve instances and explored in *Epistemology* (208), *Tendencies* (99), and *Touching Feeling* (47–48). Contemplating his "arrears," his "inward

---

15 The passage also is cited in Eve Kosofsky Sedgwick, *Touching Feeling: Affect. Pedagogy, Performativity* (Durham: Duke University Press, 2003), 22.

accumulation of material," James imagines writing as plunging his hand — indeed, his arm — deep within the "sacred and cool darkness" of his tabooed bowels, fisting himself to relieve himself of the "accumulated good stuff" that keeps on giving itself up. As Eve notes, this scene refuses the distinction of active and passive; its two-sidedness refuses dualisms. This source is founded (*au fond*) in the singularity of a pun or two. Herring traces a path whose final instantiation he oddly omits to mention. It starts in *Epistemology*, continued through a seminar at Duke that had *Wings of the Dove* on the syllabus (Michael Moon co-taught; I participated) in which Eve tried out her later reading of James, concluding in the last essay she completed before her death, "Anality: News From the Front." She never left the behind behind.

*

Herring's exploration of "fecal object relations" (7) takes him, along with Eve, to wonder whether the reparative is as far as Kleinian object relations go. "Paranoid Reading and Reparative Reading" often is taken to be Eve's last word on the subject. That 1997 essay, reprinted in *Touching Feeling*, was not the end of her thinking. "Melanie Klein and the Difference Affect Makes," ten years later, along with passages in *The Weather in Proust*, nudge object relations towards the conjunction of shit and silk. "Here and there in her writings," as Herring observes, "questions emerge into *non-Kleinian* — not just non-Lacanian — modes of being in the world that might give 'some possibilities of opening out our relation to the depressive'" (12). He pursues this speculation of Eve's in "Melanie Klein and the Difference Affect Makes" along with the recurrence of "possibilities" as a potent word in Eve's vocabulary throughout her career for the process of "opening out" (12). It characterizes what she found to think about in the texts she explored, as well as in the life she lived, facing her continuing desire not to live, finding motives to live and to create through her love and interest in others. To counter nondualistically the tally of losses that constitute our existence, he reminds us of Eve's resistance to the painful askesis of Elizabeth Bishop's "One Art" of losing, her offer, instead, of multiple arts of "loosing," a letting go that allows an expansion into "the open mesh of possibilities, gaps, overlaps, dissonances" (*Tendencies* 8) literally realized in Eve's late textile art. It's basic to her pedagogy, the most instructive scene of which is perhaps the one she recounts in *Touching Feeling*. She faints, passes out; her self-absenting could "wrench the boundaries of discourse round in productive if not always obvious ways," she proposes (34). Being beside herself in this way, opened out, splayed, Eve figures the enjambed position of "beside" she affirms in relation to the dualisms fostered by the more familiar conceptual relations of behind, before, beyond.

*

Herring's speculations about possibilities beside the depressive draw on the discussion of the topic by Lauren Berlant and Lee Edelman in *Sex, or the Unbearable*, developed from a dialogue delivered at the 2010 MLA convention. Berlant questions Edelman's demonstration that Eve's attempts to open out the reparative always involves negations that, he contends, lead her back to paranoid splitting. He insists that her "and" is an alibi for "or." Berlant continually concedes his point, as it relates to her "cruel optimism," but also resists it, most promisingly when she ponders the non-necessity that possibility opens. What is possible, after all, is not certain. It escapes epistemological determination. Indeed, for something to remain possible it must not yet be or at least not be apprehended as such. It exists as the non-existent possibility of possibility, a perpetual state of non-being and not-knowing. She wonders if Edelman's eternal "no" might be nudged in this direction of "the Sedgwickian nonce."[16] She has in mind the "nonce taxonomy" of *Epistemology* (23). It is arguably recalled in Eve's embrace of non-being in "Making Things, Practicing Emptiness." Affectively, we have seen examples of this stance when, for instance, Eve met the dread of death with

---

16 Lauren Berlant and Lee Edelman, *Sex, Or the Unbearable* (Durham: Duke University Press, 2013), 55.

newfound interests and energy. It would be difficult to call this response merely reparative since it was less about making new wholes, more an affirmation of a multiplicity of motives all at once. Nothing is excluded in these nonce solutions; even Edelman's dualistic "no" might be folded into it.

It's worth noting, too, as Berlant does, that sex returns in these possibilities, albeit in loosened, non-individualized forms of extended relationality. Such possibilities participate in Eve's breathtaking list of what "beside" includes: "a wide range of desiring, identifying, representing, repelling, paralleling, differentiating, rivalry, tearing, twisting, mimicry, withdrawing, attracting, aggressing, warping, and other relations" (*Touching Feeling* 8). It's not that "and" is a series of "or's"; "and" and "or" belong in a series of relations in which sameness and difference are preserved and mooted in the space of possibilities. In her art of loosing, Eve writes, "ideally, life, love, and ideas might then sit freely, for a while, in the palm of the open hand" (3). What we hold on to now is made possible by the realization of life that continues in our absence, in our being in non-being, surviving, living on. This is how the universe lives and we in it, how "the things in it, including oneself and one's contents" live (*Weather in Proust* 32). It is impossible not to hear — that is, it is possible to hear — in the rephrasing of "oneself" and "one's contents," the "fecal object relations" of Scott Herring's "other objects."

*

The thoughts pursued in "Eve Sedgwick's 'Other Materials'" follow from a close reading of "Bathroom Song," its trajectory from the personal to the impersonal. Herring notes for instance the many ways in which the opening stanzas identify the "I" of the poem with the biographical Eve Kosofsky: the precocity of her toilet training, her childhood home in Dayton, Ohio, her supportive parents recognizing their gifted, precocious child even in her potty offerings. The final stanza analogizes these scenes with a citation from the Heart Sutra. It keeps with the biographical evidence of Eve's engagement with Buddhism. Nonetheless, in the representation of the infant Eve by the adult writing the poem, the "I," in Herring's reading, moves to occupy two positions at once; her anal matter comes to occupy the position of "impersonal matter, Eve Kosofsky Sedgwick as 'other materials'" (10). The precocious one-year-old "outstrips conventional timelines," he continues; this "I" is finally, and at first, "a piece of matter that belongs to no one and everyone but the universe" (9). Grandma Frieda in the poem is perhaps the grandmother from whom Eve learned the weaver's handshake, the grasp of texture that locates oneself peacefully outside oneself. Herring's reading situates the text's echoes of previous texts as an impersonal extension. It is akin to Buddhist prayer flags that message themselves on the wind and water. In "Bathroom Song," Eve's bodily waste arrives at the ear of her grandmother, and of God, as well as the cave of Memory (the Henry James scenario; a Proustian scene too). Grandmother is echoed in the face of her son, Eve's father. Eve, bald like him, is transgendered. Renaming herself Evita draws attention to the meaning of "Eve" in Genesis through its translation into a proper foreign name — "Eve" means life, Being that is. As Herring recalls, the poem first appeared in "Come As You Are," title of a Nirvana hit that became a byword of its time, inviting its audience to come any way it wants to be, or was, or is wanted to be, as friend, as enemy, white or black, to face the possibility denied of being killed, annihilated, or kept in the refrain of memory. Herring sums up his reading as the conjunction of "a playful return to her body's *impersonal* arts and crafts ... structured around non-attachment" (14). "Bathroom Song," he concludes, "is, I remind myself, a poem" (16). That reminder reminds us of what "and" joins in the title of Eve's course: "Words and Other Materials."

*

I would put this aesthetic reminder beside Brian Glavey's *The Wallflower Avant-Garde,* a book about queer ekphrasis that takes off from the movement of Eve's thought. Rather than offering the usual bifurcated early/late Eve divided between epistemological erotic concerns and "abstract questions of affect and temporality," Glavey connects the close readings of "The Weather in Proust" (starting with the fountain in Proust as an exemplary ekphrasis) with the site of a sexiness for Eve that she located early, as she recounts in *Tendencies* and reiterated thereafter: "for me, a kind of formalism, a visceral near-identification with the writing I cared for, at the level of sentence structure, metrical pattern, rhyme, was one way of trying to appropriate what seemed the numinous and resistant power of the chosen objects" (*Tendencies* 3). In that becoming-object lies an impersonal mode of attachment to the world, "seeing something as itself and something else at the same time."[17]

Glavey posits a non-dualistic reading of Eve's oeuvre. Rethinking her own rethinking, he arrives at the creativity that Eve celebrates, the galvanizing effects of her own self-withdrawals. "The performative utterance, according to Sedgwick, behaves much as the queer child does in her work, shyly turning inward but with electrifying effects on those drawn into her proximity" (148). Those effects are bound to the near-identifications, near-misses, with the objects that draw one, the object-relations Scott Herring identifies. "Sedgwick's meteorological turn thus should not be seen as shying away from the sexual," Glavey insists. It participates in the "wallflower avant-gardism defined in part by its reluctance to being snared in the sorts of oppositional thinking that would pitch the antisocial and the utopian as opposites" (3). Eve's aestheticism is both a mode of attachment and detachment. Nonce-relations allow one for a time to survive fastened to what remains when we have parted from this world — the world itself and what we may have added to it by having been here for a while.

*

---

17 Brian Glavey, *The Wallflower Avant-Garde: Modernism, Sexuality, and Queer Ekphrasis* (Oxford: Oxford University Press, 2016), 3.

Arriving here we approach the conjunction that Judith Butler offers in her contribution to *Reading Sedgwick* (a reworking of yet another talk originally delivered at the 2010 MLA convention). "Proust at the End" is a doubled end in which Eve and Barbara Johnson meet. Both died within months of each other; both were reading Proust at the end. They read him, Butler argues, for the kind of "posthumous happiness" that Swann is said to have achieved in marrying Odette, a woman for whom he has no desire except the desire to live past attachment and its attendant jealousy, to live in the life that outlives our own. "Posthumous happiness," in Butler's analysis, entails proliferating the self through "connections among humans and things"; "It is about being determined in relation to others and to an ambient world."[18] Eve and Barbara, she supposes, both enjoyed this other way of loving. "Who among us is *not* in love with Barbara Johnson," Judy reports Eve as having said. Affirming her own love for them both, she closes by claiming "that something about that other way of loving is what is happening still …. We took her in," she writes, about Eve, "and breathe her still, with surprise, and with gratitude" (70).

*

Butler's conclusion brings me back to "Eve Sedgwick's 'Other Materials,'" to something I might have remarked on earlier, its dedication to me and Michael Moon. Until Scott sent us a copy of his published essay we had no idea he was writing it or dedicating it to us. We have known Scott since his partner Shane Vogel had a post-doc at Emory University's humanities center in 2006, but were not involved in his writing of the essay. We are the dedicatees, I think, the way we are in the essay, thanks to our relationships with Eve, especially our writing-relations (my editing *The Weather in Proust,* Michael's co-authoring "Divinity"). As Scott indicates movingly at several moments in his

---

18 Judith Butler, "Proust at the End," in *Reading Sedgwick,* ed. Lauren Berlant (Durham: Duke University Press, 2019), 69.

essay, he never knew Eve; yet he writes, he hopes, without being misconstrued, of matters intimate to her, matters she shared, of course, in writing. "Her writings have been formative to my own writing on queer matters as well as my development as a white, gay male who came to US queer theory with Sedgwick's work in my pocket" (7). This is how he positions himself early in his essay. He ends it this way: "So thank the powers that be for Little Evita's ode de toilette. Schooled at the University of Illinois at Urbana-Champaign, I was unable to take one of her classes, but these are a few of the queer things that reading up on Sedgwick's waste materials — from her earliest to her latest on "BUDDHIST STUFF" — brought to my mind for this journal's special issue on queer objects. Treat this piece as a belated going-away gift for all the intimate stuff she never meant to give me, even though Sedgwick and I had absolutely no personal relationship whatsoever" (16).

Scott's expression of gratitude here sounds like Judith Butler's, except that it is offered without the personal knowledge of Eve and Barbara Johnson that Butler had; Eve's writing is a gift not intended for him but nonetheless received by him in the personal/impersonal exchange that writing affords across the abyssal divide in objects detached and attached to ourselves as our selves are attached to/detached from shit, silk, bodies, words, things.

"Come As You Are"

Eve's talk was first delivered at a conference on death and dying at SUNY Stony Brook in November 1999. She gave it in conjunction with an exhibit of her fabric art titled "Floating Columns/ In the Bardo." I turn to the talk prompted by Scott Herring's brilliant attention to a central, material aspect of Eve's focus on the realization of her own mortality. Her "Bathroom Song" guides him, and Eve ends "Come As You Are" by quoting it. He didn't know its original position and put forward what she put behind. This forward/backward conjunction fits the position of the "I" of the poem, as he noted: the infant Eve cannot be distinguished from its dying author. So, too, with fecal matter: it begins in food removed from its organic existence that we need to live; eliminated as waste, it becomes mulch that replenishes soil. The cycle continues. The meeting of beginning and ending is where we are to come as we are. After.

"I'll end with one more poem — this one's about toilet training, but it, too, quotes from the Heart Sutra," Eve concludes. "Death" is the other poem of hers to which she alludes. She quotes it in full and recalls lines from it at several points. "Come-as-you-are" appears in its second line. Eve quotes "The point's not what becomes you, but what's you," as she concludes. "Becomes" suggests at once "what makes you look best," as well as "what you will turn into." The two are connected, fabrics might adorn your body, but like other objects, including your body, they must be let go. The floating figures exhibited in Eve's bardo — headless, lacking hands and feet — are made of fabric, covered in Eve's textiles, fabric inside and out.

Connections between what you are and what becomes you are pursued throughout "Come As You Are" as Eve repeatedly asks who/what am I? "Why textiles, why Buddhism?" Why did these "come bounding" into her life as she came to realize her mortality? This, she insists, is and remains a real question, demurring from the usual stance of authorial control that would strive to make it seem as if the arguments and connections in her writing were "overdetermined." To Eve, they remain "underdetermined." These two terms — and the either/or they might suppose — are woven into the discussion at every turn, posing its central quandary. The overdetermined "we all must die" that we all know is joined to but disjunct from the undetermined "we don't know how or when." Even Eve's realization of her own death stops short there. The self, its capacity to master situations, is implicated. We live with a knowledge that we barely realize. Eve ponders the moment of realization — "It was the time when I learned that the breast cancer for which I'd been treated half-a-dozen years earlier had silently metastasized to my spine, and had become incurable" (this sentence comes well into "Reality and Realization" but at the beginning of "Come As

You Are") — ponders it because the ongoing realization of her mortality may make it more real, or perhaps not. Nor can she determine the order of events that precipitated the conjunction of fabrics and Buddhism. Which came first, and was it before or after the diagnosis? Such determinations remain indeterminate, underdetermined. Rather than being able to answer the questions she can only wonder. Questions about temporality and life, raised at the opening of the talk, recur at its close. Eve reports that she has "come to terms" with "a process where endless underdeterminations continue to arise and arise in the face of one single overdetermination, whose narrative coherence will be only retrospective." She has come to the end of questions about ends and determinations, left with what arises and arises, a phrase that may remind us of Henry James's fantasy.

"What are these things doing in my *life*? I mean *my* life?" Textiles and Buddhism come "bounding," violating the boundaries designated by the italicized terms. They come as things, arriving like the silently metastasizing cancer. Eve opposes the usual way of thinking of disease as an enemy to be combated, some undisciplined, immature, unruly, antisocial force — an outsider. Without saying more, she closes by making clear that fatal disease often is treated the same way as perverse sexuality is stigmatized. She advocates acceptance of what is, of what we are.

"Come As You Are" begins with what appears to be a sidebar in an opening paragraph about the slide show that accompanied the talk, but was not "particularly synchronized with it," offering, she stresses, a variety of images of various Buddhisms and various textile traditions, each with its own modes of representation.[19] The images, she continues, form "a sort of musical background or light show." They are in a relation of ekphrastic exchange, two arts at once. As a light show, they show what makes them visible, what they are, not merely what they represent. The light show thus illuminates the quandary posed by the italicized terms *my life* (whose *life* is *my* life?). Buddhist practices of real-

---

19 Hal Sedgwick, who ran the projector, informs me that he showed somewhere around four hundred slides during the delivery of the talk.

ization tend in this direction as well, as does work in textiles that push back against the maker. In the bardo of death (Dharmata, the bardo of reality) "we can recognize the impersonal luminosity of mind …, recognize it not only as itself but *as ourselves* and not other than ourselves." The light show mentioned as if it were an opening aside anticipates what comes after death. (The passages in "Reality and Realization" on the bardo light shows come in the middle of "Come As You Are.") At such a moment, "the individuating, inexorable, karmic laws of dualistic cause and effect will be transformed into, or simply recognized as, the overarching, radically underdeterminimg, transpersonal freedom called realization."

"The point's not what becomes you, but what's you." In "Death" the "I" asks, "Why did I buy those silk PJs, with feathers / so long before the big affair began? / I've always slept in the nude. Now I sleep in the nude forever." "Always" becomes "forever"; "Now" is the time in which this "I" speaks, a time that survives it. It has become what it is, an "I" in a text that illuminates what touching a textile intimates, "a reality, a beauty, that wasn't myself, wasn't any self, and didn't want to be" that Eve "hungers" to handle. It answers the question "Death" poses. Not wanting to be is how to be. "No one sends the message … no one receives" it; this no one is you, neither sender nor receiver, subject nor object. No one yet not split in two either. What is written in the wind is something untraceable, evanescent as the moment. It is a matter of forgetting tantamount to realization.

"Reality and Realization" had intimated the co-implication of remembering and forgetting (maternal injunctions, rules of hospitality and exchange). "Come As You Are" furthers the discussion. Seriously joking, Eve wonders where her memory has gone, whether everyone's has, presciently anticipating a present in which our memories are stored in our devices and tweets replace thoughts. Quietly demurring from a point in Sogyal Rinpoche's *Tibetan Book of Living and Dying* (quoted far more extensively in this talk than in "Reality and Realization"), in which he posits the discovery of a true self against the ego to which we cling as if it were ourselves. Forgetting, rather, is key to the not-self one is; making things invests one in "*things* [that] neither have nor are opinions and, ideally, cannot be mistaken for them." They have no egos. When we make them (to the extent they permit) they return us to what we otherwise forget we are. In "The Weather in Proust," Eve links forgetting to platonism and neoplatonism, anamnesis and Plotinian meditation, to the re-minding that is realized in the little gods (cupids) that populate Proust's landscape and beckon towards the other scene beside the one we know as our familiar reality, relations other than the clinging repudiations of desire and jealousy; those imprisonments. Memoria, memoria.

Eve reports herself "annealed into that instant in time," the moment of realization. Fused with it, she is, at the same time shattered, unraveled. She is in what is forgotten, mindful in mindlessness. Characteristically, at the end of her talk, she wonders anew and asks again what she asked at the beginning, "Why the object fixation onto fiber art as *real*? Forget underdetermination; what can the sublimity of forgetting have to do with the hyper-retentiveness of these 'schmatta studies'?" Are these not transitional objects? Asked and answered: are we not ourselves transitional objects? Think back to our investment in security blankets, worn away by our clinging to them, covered in tears and other bodily excretions; go back to toilet training. "Why would it be a scandal if the task of dying and those of toddlerhood such as individuation and even toilet training were not so different — were, so to speak, molded of the same odorous, bimorphic clay." These provocative questions lead to the discussion of self and not self, of waste products and letting go, the conjunction of shit and satin. The "scandal" of existence lies in its nondualistic doubleness: we are part of what we leave behind, palpably connected to what is not us. These connections across ontological divides also characterize sexuality. In "Death," we are told how to (un)dress for the party, the affair with death. We are addressed as "man" by a speaker whose body worries seem to include a tummy that needs girdling and elevator shoes to add height. Is the "man" so colloquially addressed male or female? Is the speaker? "Suppose the many, stubborn, transformational negotiations with chosen cloth objects are a medium for experimenting with the dimensions and new possibilities of this unwelcome imperative" of "letting go." Eve realized this in figures floating in the bardo.

Same and different, two and one, beginning and end. Eve entertains the unwelcome imperative of death. She returns at the end of her talk to Rick Fields, mentioned earlier in the context of the kind of academic project that opened "Reality and Realization," and that Eve mentions two thirds of the way into "Come As You Are." Fields explored American (white) Buddhism, now he is invoked for how he approached death — his death — as a way of life, finding where he was "on the cycle of existence" that joins beginning and ending. We are all living dying. To realize that is to find where we are and who we are. Eve likens this discovery to the conjunction of AIDS and cancer that had occupied her at least from *Tendencies* on. They join to create new forms of relation between persons, genders, races, opening new public spaces. On a personal level, in this "now," Eve is both terminal and alive, doing well and dying, entering thereby into a new realms of freedom "both of meaning, relation, and memory, yet also from them." By not holding onto what one must let go of, one could identify lovingly with *it,* "identify," Eve writes, "with the fabric and structure of this discohesive fate itself." To illustrate this, take "Bathroom Song." Follow one's shit across boundaries to be "utterly gone" into "enlightenment,"

> Send the sucker off to Grandma
> Gaté, gaté, paragaté;
> parasamgaté; bodhi; svaha!

We arrive at the end of "Come As You Are" where Scott Herring began; this is where Eve ends and where we (and she) come after when we come as we are.

"Woven Spaces"

My heading comes from the title of the first of two essays on Eve's work by Katy Hawkins. "Woven Spaces: Eve Kosofsky Sedgwick's *Dialogue on Love*" appeared in the same issue of *Women and Performance* that included the two poems quoted in "Come As You Are." "Re-Creating Eve: Sedgwick's Art and the Practice of Renewal" is the printed version of the talk that Katy (here named Katherine) gave at the Honoring Eve Symposium at Boston University on October 31, 2009. Katy Hawkins was a dissertation student of Eve's at the CUNY Graduate Center and, as she notes in both essays, intended to publish a book on Eve's creative career. She situates both essays around occasions in her relationship with Eve.

The first is set at SUNY Stony Brook in 1999 when Eve delivered "Come As You Are." Katy's mother, the author of a book on illness, also was there; Katy introduced the two women. In her essay, she compares their ways of understanding illness and death. She extends notions of maternity through a key passage in *Dialogue of Love* (217) in which the encounter of Aeneas and his mother Venus applies to the positions occupied by Eve and Shannon Van Wey as much as it does to whoever is reading/receiving her words. Within this widening matrix, Katy poignantly ends her essay by noting how this extended relation prepares us for loss, as Aeneas is when he retrospectively recognizes the goddess guiding him: "We must gaze at such gifts long enough to realize them, so that we can be okay when she is gone."[20]

This final sentence locates "Woven Spaces" in the matrix of the "after" that is my concern. An essay that begins with a personal encounter becomes an exchange much like the one that ends Scott Herring's essay. The gift of Eve's work, enmeshed with a recall of Virgil, in dialogue with Anne Hunsaker Hawkins's *Reconstructing Illness: Studies in Pathography,* extends into the capacious freedom of the impersonal; it is exemplified and

---

20 Katy Hawkins, "Woven Spaces: Eve Kosofsky Sedgwick's 'Dialogue on Love,'" *Women and Performance* 16, no. 2 (July 2006): 266.

made available in Eve's "art and practice of renewal," to recall the subtitle of "Re-creating Eve." Midway through it, the title describes Eve's practice and ours, she mentions that in her talk she has discussed Eve's art works in the order in which Eve first showed them to her. Her essay recreates her experience. We are surprised to discover that we don't know to whose agency we should ascribe its movement from beginning to end.

These two essays are among the most capacious and suggestive writings to explore the full range of Eve's creative output. "Woven spaces" is but one figure offered to summarize the double movement of an opening that affords all kinds of crossings. "Nexus," "matrix," "knot," and "tangle" are other terms for the time/space explored. From the first sentence of "Re-Creating Eve," in which she looks forward to the publication of "The Weather in Proust," which she has read already, the motives of renewal, refreshment and recreation project an "after" into a future we may inhabit, a time/space where we may be, where we are, in relation to Eve's oeuvre unfolded in the essay. In what follows I trace only a few of these salient conjunctions.

*

One of the ambitions of these essays is to articulate relationships between early and late Eve. In the precis to "Woven Spaces," she writes that in *Dialogue on Love* "Sedgwick's approach … develops the theoretical concepts from across her oeuvre," immediately glancing at the "historical, formal and theoretical matrices" involved (251). From the start, even before the essay has begun, it weaves its threads. Its matrix cannot really be confined to a singular topic or account when the strands that come together expand to encompass such concerns as "nonlinear time, hybrid form, and intersubjective relation." By the end of the precis, a text first said to develop concepts is redescribed "as an important extension of her scholarship." This development might as easily be called a transformation. At the same time, when couched as a matter of "intersubjective relation," we have to note that the essay argues that Eve faced terminal illness as she had always faced her life: she never supposed her own bodily or subjective integrity.

The concept that links early and late Sedgwick in "Woven Spaces" is "queer." The term is attached to Eve's subjectivity "as an open space for multiple temporal positions" (253; she is both herself and not herself), to the mixed form of *Dialogue* (poetry and prose, for starters, Eve's "I" and Shannon's in their own typeface, but not subjectively separate). It extends to Melanie Klein's work: "Reparative motives seem to 'rhyme' with Eve's prior theorization of queer ones," Howkins writes (256). "Seem," as well as the metaphoric use of "rhyme," suggest at once similarity and difference as a way to describe these temporal relations. In Eve's turn to the reparative (paired with the paranoid), she also sees "a shift away from anxious, fixated obsession toward a kind of detached, curious, relishing interest" that "revives creative interest ... generating space for the interplay of multiple positions and identifications." This detachment creates "a gap between the present reconstructing self and the past experiencing selves" (256). Although that gap might suggest an interruption, a break between past and present, it also is the space of renewed creativity. True to Eve's thought, Hawkins reformulates either/or versus both/and as either/or and both/and.

A couple of footnotes in "Re-Creating Eve" glance at continuities from early to late Sedgwick. Space, one metaphor for what Eve's work opens as well as the realized terrain it occupies, is sketched in note 4. This theme, she writes, becomes "more overt": from *The Coherence of Gothic Fiction* to the treatment of texture in *Touching Feeling*, a difference within the same emerges, a developmental narrative that still leaves in question the relationship between knowing and realizing. The covert/overt plot posits a realization of a truth not so much about who one is as it is about what is.

Another continuity is pursued in note 9, the "analogy of weaving for writing (and, indeed, thinking)" across Eve's work.[21]

---

21 Katherine Hawkins, "Re-Creating Eve: Sedgwick's Art and the Practice of Renewal," *Criticism* 52, no. 2 (Spring 2010): 281.

This note glosses the late loom book Eve made in which threads and strips of treated fiber create a multidimensional space across which, in various alphabetical shapes, clauses from Proust are deployed. "As such, the Loom Book is the very definition of Queer work, according to Sedgwick's definition in *Tendencies*." The passage she has in mind also is crucial for Jason Edwards in "For Beauty Is a Series of Hypotheses?: Sedgwick as Fiber Artist." It is the one in which Eve defines "one of the things that 'queer' can refer to: the open mesh of possibilities, gap, overlap, dissonances and resonances, lapses and excesses of meaning when the constituent elements of anyone's gender, of anyone's sexuality aren't made (or *can't* be made) to signify monolithically" (*Tendencies* 8; recall that Fawaz titles his introduction to *Reading Sedgwick* "An Open Mesh of Possibilities").

"Mesh," "gap": Eve's first two terms are drawn from weaving, a coming together that also is a temporal spacing apart; the next phrases, joined by "and" bring together what might usually be separated as contradictory. "Elements," a bit further on, deploys a word that could designate the basic materials out of which all things are made as well as the letters that form words — what we learn in elementary school. All things are made only in positions/relations. The letters of the alphabet are arbitrary strokes meant to mean. Eve's most immediate reference is to the categories of identity — gendered, sexual — that either refuse to signify singularly or that are refused that capacity. That refusal — those refusals — nonetheless can be drawn under the capacious rubric of "queer" since it brings together all things athwart, cross-woven. Eve is not finished defining "queer" in this sentence. The next paragraph zooms in to "same-sex object choice, lesbian or gay" as "the term's definitional center," while the paragraph that follows, "at the same time" zooms out to "dimensions that can't be subsumed under gender and sexuality: all the ways that race, ethnicity, postcolonial nationality crisscross with these *and other* identity-constituting, identity-fracturing discourses, for example" (9). The definitional centers of "queer" are at once an "open mesh of possibilities" that also may inhere to the specificity of an orientation.

Open possibilities stand in relation to what seems closed. Eve's loom book realizes that: it is incapable of being read the way the phrases in Proust's text would be in their sequential encounter in a book. The text in the loom has no determinate order. In "Making Things, Practicing Emptiness," Eve analyzes the enforcements of language, sentences, including Proust's extravagantly long ones, that posit subjects and objects in a determinate grammatical order. These sentences, moreover, appear to come from a source, an author, and create a subordinate position for the reader (*Weather in Proust* 79, 105). Things evade, open up, these positions of propositional knowledge, the domain of writing. Eve's trajectory in "Making Things" parallels a quandary posed by this relation. She begins as if weaving were a refusal of writing, but ends insisting that there was no way for her to exclude writing from her weaving. Moreover, despite the eastern influence on her craft — binding Buddhism to textiles bound to her life — Proust persisted, a long-held love, as textiles were too. Both preceded her realization of mortality: they went from being a means of self-adornment, self-enhancement, self-preservation, to becoming her way to self-abandonment.

In "Re-Creating Eve," Hawkins considers Eve's relation to Proust: "her art is perhaps the best place to see the contours not just of the Proust she recasts for us, but of the late Sedgwickian mode she simultaneously refines." "Recasts" and "refines" are the final verbs in this paragraph used to describe the arc of Eve's career, the "expansive movement in her oeuvre from the propositional mode of knowingness in, for example, *Between Men* and *Epistemology* towards a drive in her later work towards themes of refreshment and rebirth" (278). These formulations, even as they posit differences between early and late also pose them in reiterative relations. Indeed, if one glances at the final chapter of *Epistemology*, "Proust and the Spectacle of the Closet," one can see resonances, anticipations of late in early, as Eve explores the contradictions between Proust's reductive statements about homosexuality in book four of the *Recherche* and the figuration that conveys and exceeds this propositional content. The closet in Proust is multiple, deployed as much as a spectacle supposedly to be seen through as a space in which hiding is a losing game. Reading the "glass closet" of Charlus involves a "volatile barometric career," Eve writes (*Epistemology* 228), deploying a figure that will become an index to the weather in Proust. Throughout she is on the lookout for "enabling nexuses of incoherence in the text" (226), knots that unravel the choking constriction of the laws of desire. These are, as Hawkins writes, the "typical weather" in Proust, closed systems that seem closed; Eve "assembles an entirely new Proust" from his "unmatched skill for reawakening the vitality of the world" ("Re-Creating Eve" 277). The "entirely new" is not located somewhere other than in the deadening old.

Arguably, there is a path from the deconstructive strategies of *Epistemology* to Eve's later work. Her move to making things did not mean that she stopped writing. Eve balks in *Touching Feeling* at the infinitizing evacuations of anti-essentialism, not in order to reinstate essentialism but to find something beside it, an eastern notion of fullness coincident with emptiness, a continuum across the ontological divide of life and death located in Being (and also in the verb "to be"), a reality principle in which the end of anyone's life, that terminus, coincides with the realization of death possible in life. Despite the emphasis on dying and the afterlife in the first books Eve read about Buddhism, Sogyal Rinpoche's and Robert Thurman's recensions of Tibetan explorations of the bardos, these books also can re-orient one to how to live. Rather than proclaiming that there is nothing but text, these show how nothing will come of nothing. "Deconstruction is the theory, Buddhism is the practice," is Eve's formulation in "Making Things, Practicing Emptiness" (*Weather in Proust* 75).

*

To return to the queer weave of *Tendencies*, a page before the passage Hawkins cites, Eve anticipates the definitions she offers there: "What if ... there were a practice of valuing the ways in which meanings and institutions can be at loose ends with each other? What if the richest junctures weren't the ones where *ev-*

erything means the same thing?" What if they didn't "line up" (6)? The line is reimagined as a juncture, a crossing in which things pass over and beside each other, like changing trains in a terminal, cleaving together and apart, in a passage that is also a knot, the way to what is not self, letting go. The result is raveled selvage, loose ends of the kind Eve left in her weaving, as Jason Edwards notes. They mark the materiality of transversed boundaries. What is it to be at loose ends? To be in a state of mind in which one's habits and routines are interrupted by an unfamiliar emptiness: boredom, anxiety, excitement; to be at loose ends also is an activity, or so the supposed origin of the phrase suggests. Sailors, when they had a spare moment, were enjoined to check the ropes to make sure there were no loose ends that might scuttle the ship. To tighten them or to let go?

*

Retrospectively, as we noted, we are told that "Re-Creating Eve" was shaped by the order in which Eve showed Katy her art. First comes a piece in which words from Proust are placed on the body parts of flexible mannikins that fly through the space of a watercolor background, a "matrix" that corresponds to the breath of Proust's narrator's grandmother that offers an "infinity of space" to his "constricted heart."[22] This text metamorphoses in the Loom Book citation of the recall of the first visit to Balbec recalled in "The Intermittencies of the Heart" section of *Sodom and Gomorrah,* the moment when involuntarily recalling his grandmother's death shakes the narrator's supposition "that all our inner wealth, our past joys, all our sorrows, are perpetually in our possession" (4:211); rather, our dispossession brings us to what is perpetual. Annihilation meets recreation. Language pulses with its self-undoing. Hawkins illuminates the situation

---

22 Marcel Proust, *In Search of Lost Time,* 6 vols., trans. C.K. Scott Moncrieff and Terence Kilmartin (New York: Modern Library, 2003), 2:334. Further references to Proust in my text will be to volume and page number in this edition.

with an etymology: "Sutra: Sanskrit for 'thread'" ("Re-Creating Eve" 276). Sutras are detachable bits, aphoristic condensations embedded in longer texts. "Each thread is designed to be examined as a free, isolated unit and at the same time the fabric of the whole is to be respected" (276). You can pick up a thread at any point, the order of the text is not its only order. Buddhism and weaving came bounding into Eve's life at the moment of the realization of death in the way that "sutra" weaves together text and thread.

The last image in "Re-Creating Eve" features Guanyin, the Boddhisatva of Compassion, in triplicate with a Proust text set beside the statue in two of its iterations: "As in the classical landscapes where in the place of a vanished nymph there is an inanimate spring, a discernible and concrete intention had been transformed into a certain limpidity of tone, strange, appropriate and cold" (Proust 3:55). Cold: the inhospitality of the indifferent, impersonal universe, as in Woolf, *The Waves*, "We are cut. … We become part of that unfeeling universe."[23] Proust's analogy is one of several offered to describe the effect of the voice of the consummate actress Berma, "which the fascinated spectator … took not for a triumph of dramatic artistry but for a manifestation of life" (3:55). Guanyin is insistently worldly, as Hawkins emphasizes, Eve, too, toward the conclusion of "Making Things" when she describes Guanyin's reserve and accessibility as "relational … but not interpersonal," an embodiment of the Heart Sutra's "not self, not other, not both self and other, and not neither self nor other" (*Weather in Proust* 104). "And 'similar,'" Eve continues, "seems to me to characterize their relation to gender … not male, not female, not both male and female, and not neither male nor female" (105). A queer conclusion.

Svaha. With that word, Katy closes her journey through the images Eve showed her. Untranslatable word at the end of "Bathroom Song" and the Heart Sutra, it resonates with Eve's parsing of the compactions of "thusness" in "Pedagogy of Buddhism,"

---

23 Virginia Woolf, *The Waves* (New York: Harcourt, Brace and Co., 1931), 280.

where she writes, "the double movement of an apperceptive attraction to phenomena in all their immeasurable, inarticulable specificity, and at the same time an evacuation of the apparent ontological grounds of that specificity and, indeed, their being. The endless vibrancy of this resonant double movement …" (*Touching Feeling* 171). A sentence from Proust can be put beside Guanyin because, as Eve noted in her statement about "Works in Fiber, Paper, and Proust," Proust's language and thought is a medium like paper or fabric. It can "reflect the transformative potential of prolonged immersion in someone else's mental world." To be "in" Proust is to experience a holding environment, "simple material metamorphoses [of daily life] as they are emulsified with language and meaning" (*Weather in Proust* 120–21). "Emulsified" allows for both separation and meeting, the material doubleness of what is.

Buddhist thought, as both of Katy Hawkins's essays show over and again, provides the matrix for the final metamorphoses in Eve's formulations in her writing and weaving. Such coming together, taking apart is expressed this way by Sogyal Rinpoche:

> Nothing has any *inherent* existence of its own when you really look at it, and this absence of independent existence is what we call "emptiness." Think of a tree. When you think of a tree, you tend to think of a distinctly defined object; and on a certain level, like a wave, it is. But when you look more closely at the tree, you will see that ultimately it has no independent existence. When you contemplate it, you will find that it dissolves into an extremely subtle net of relationships that stretches across the universe.[24]

In this passage, the existence of individual objects (the tree, the self) is admitted, but as an open mesh of possibilities created by the crossing and intersections of a reality that passes through it, giving it the potential to be and to go on being. These remain

---

24 Soygal Rinpoche, *The Tibetan Book of Living and Dying* (New York: HarperCollins, 2002), 37.

possible only by not being entirely realized. Realization, the fullness of what is, remains a potential necessarily empty, ready to be filled, resonant. Sogyal Rinproche's language is metaphorical. The tree is likened to a wave (once again, I can't help but recall Virginia Woolf), elements cross in a "subtle net" of relationships. The tree can't be fully divorced from what makes it live, yet what gives it life denies it "inherent existence." What holds it together is like the glue in a collage or stitch-binding fabrics that marks separation as does every boundary in a collage. "It can never be said too often that to realize the nature of mind is to realize the nature of things," Sogyal Rinpoche writes (*Tibetan Book* 48). Even mind is matter, material that is the basis for what Eve called Proust's mysticism, "the beings in the universe are filled … with the stuff *of* the universe" (*Weather in Proust* 32).

*

"May not thought itself be part of reality as a whole?," the physicist David Bohm asks.[25] Eve devotes a couple of pages to Bohm in "Making Things, Practicing Emptiness" (*Weather in Proust* 100–101) and alludes to him again at the end of the chapter. For Bohm, wholeness requires a rethinking of the whole/part relationship like that found in Buddhist thought. Eve's understanding of "thusness" arises from contemplating a version of it in the finger/moon relationship of the index and the object it points. They are co-dependent. Eve notices Bohm's favored terms to describe this relationship, implicate and explicate; their internal fold resonates with a technique in her fabric art, *shibori* tie-dye, fabric folded and opened to show new dimensions. The image Eve chose to exemplify this in "Works in Fiber, Paper, and Proust" (fig. 16; *Weather in Proust*) knots together fabric on each end; sentences from Proust appear on the cloth; gathered they form a new object. It exists as such but also as something to be taken in, to the extent it can be, by eyes and mind. In shibori

---

25 David Bohm, *Wholeness and the Implicate Order* (London: Routledge, 1980), xi.

"the connection between the folded and unfolded ... states ... is very intimate, but ... the ... states don't look even remotely alike" (98). For Bohm this is true of the relationship between the implicate and explicate states of the universe, joined in the movement of reservoirs of energy from which all discrete things come and into which they go, endlessly, in a time/space whose dimensionality is immeasurable.

Here it helps to recall that "eternity" and "infinity" are negative concepts. It is in negation, in nothing, that relation takes place. Bohm offers no comprehensive propositional theory to explain everything but offers a transformational relation between two orders whose lack of likeness does not preclude their sameness: "in its totality, the holomovement is not limited in any specifiable way at all. It is not required to conform to any particular order, or to be bounded by any particular measure. Thus, *the holomovement is undefinable and immeasurable*" (*Wholeness and the Implicate Order* 191).

"Holomovement" is Bohm's term for the (non)relationship between a hologram and its object, a nonrepresentational model for Bohm for a whole/part relation grounded in emptiness and negativity. "Everything implicates everything," nothing *is*, except in the movement of implication and explication, of unconsciousness and attention to a part that only can be grasped when it folds back into the ungraspable. Bohm's theory derives from quantum physics, and its bottom line is "non-continuity, non-causality and non-locality" combined with "undivided wholeness" (223). Speculative, ungraspable: propositional terms govern Newtonian physics that explain the ordinary reality of the explicit; specific concretizations and perceptions make visible what makes them possible but not inherent or permanent; possibility arises and arises from the implicate order, an "immense 'sea' of energy" (243) whose governing laws remain unknown and "probably unknowable" (226). This energy joins implicate and explicate together/apart "on the basis of a single ground" (245) of materiality, where "the holomovement which is 'life implicit' is the ground both of 'life explicit' and of 'inanimate matter'" (247). Being and Non-Being meet in possibility.

*

Eve ends "Making Things, Practicing Emptiness" with the Loom Book that Katy offers as her penultimate example. The order of the images is not their point. This is perhaps conveyed by the penultimate image in Eve's talk, a band of five Boddhisatva heads, moving from fully illuminated to dark encasement, punctuated with a sentence from Proust broken into words and phrases, seven rows of marbled letters at right angle to the heads. "The most exclusive love for a person is always a love for something else" (2:563). Eve made this one for Michael and me (it's above our living room mantle). It resonates with Eve's discovery of Shannon Van Wey's care for her that Katy discusses at the end of "Woven Spaces," where Eve writes "I love that his care for me was not care for *me*" (*Dialogue* 219). Eve trips on the way to an appointment with Shannon, dislodging a patch of earth. After her session, unseen, Eve watches Shannon going over the same ground, noticing the displaced clod of mulch, patting it back where it belongs. Like the voice lodged in Eve's mind it intimates that it's time to let go, to let be.

After (again)

Proust's title, *In Search of Lost Time,* suggests a forward motion (*à la recherche*) towards recovery. It is after what lies behind, it comes after what it is after. *Recherche* is both retrospective and reiterative; *temps perdu* offers similar aporias. Can one find what has been lost? Not in Proust's terms since involuntary memory cannot be a matter of voluntary, willed, action. Whatever is found coincides with what was lost. Such a search is potentially endless. The structure of Proust's massive novel is recursive, leaving the reader with the question whether the text we have read is the book the author feels ready to write at the end of *Time Regained* or a prelude to the novel imagined there. The novel seeks to unearth what is buried, in the past, in the mind, a hidden key to determinations, decisions, desires that, at one and the same time, seem accidental, chance occurrences. Surprises,

Eve's focus in "The Weather in Proust," are moments of refreshment and reincarnation that go hand-in-hand with inexorable and inescapable laws. The activity of the novel, intimated in its title, is suspended at the nexus of sameness and difference, the forgotten and the remembered, a holding environment in which one attends to two things at once, something and something else, something and nothing.

In "The Weather in Proust," Eve remarks on the "elastic, permeable boundaries in Proust" as particularly hospitable to "the Plotinian understanding of universal soul, reality, nous, or good that, like Buddha nature, both surrounds and animates the individual" (*Weather in Proust* 14). Eve's densely packed formulation finds support in the double meaning of "individual," its older sense of indivisibility from what one is not and its modern sense of being separated as itself. Her sentence brings together a strand of neoplatonic thought about a conceptual/moral/ontological/psychological/spiritual nexus, each aspect of which is designated by a term not equivalent to the others with which it is nonetheless grammatically equated. These multiples are extended by way of "like," a term that means similar to, but not the same as, to "Buddha nature." In it, inner and outer are indeterminately joined the way the air we breathe fills our lungs. "Nature" takes the place of soul/mind. The word that draws east and west into proximity is, perhaps, "animate." It nudges, too, in the direction of animism, maybe of Aristotle's *De Anima*. As well, its Latin title translates the Greek *psuchē*, at once mind and soul and breath.

In Eve's late work in fiber, Proust and eastern texts appear, sometimes with Buddhist images. Proust and Buddhism come together, she notes in "Making Things, Practicing Emptiness," because both "function as touchstones to [her] sense of reality" (*Weather in Proust* 113). Buddhism, a late object of interest, led her to "now realize" what she had "always found in Proust" — "always," that is, after she read him soon after finishing her PhD, as she told Stephen Barber and David Clark (*Regarding Sedgwick* 245). The temporal process of now and then is, at the same time, a realization that suspends the distance between them in an "always" that gestures towards the "reality" in which both partake and, at the same time, to which they point. This daily "mysticism" involves "material metamorphoses as they are emulsified with language and meaning" (*Weather in Proust* 113). Emulsification is an activity that brings together substances that usually can't mix. Here, this occurs in "language and meaning," a doublet that might equate those two words and might not. "Material metamorphoses" seem to be located in an ordinarily perceptible reality (cooking and digesting are two textbook examples of the process), but "mysticism" suggests the form of attention Eve calls "realization," an apprehension likely to take your breath away — and perhaps available only when that happens, though perhaps, too, in dreams, or meditation on the breath that take one to the limits of self, its permeable boundaries.

Proust brings us there, Eve notes at the end of "The Weather in Proust," through aesthetic experience, especially when Proust's narrator recognizes that his talent coincides with, and is not threatened by, an art that "is something I am not" (6:240). Being an artist involves a metamorphic reincarnation into "this being that had been reborn in me" (6:264). These late recognitions are not confined to language, and in the course of the novel this art experience is found as well in music, painting, architecture, sculpture, and acting. Proust's language, as Eve insists, is a medium, a transferential one. As Glavey shows, it is ekphrastic, and not just in the passage describing the Robert fountain with which Eve opens "The Weather in Proust." The phrase in the Vinteuil sonata, Elstir's brush strokes, indeed almost any descriptive passage in the novel, filled with likes, as thoughs and as ifs, conveys the reality that draws Eve.

*

Before the narrator arrives at his understanding of his talent, Bergotte is the writer in the novel whose work intimates this impersonal understanding; I turn to him now, although late in *Within a Budding Grove,* where the title metaphorizes young women as flowers, *en fleur,* the painter Elstir takes over the role that Bergotte plays earlier. Elstir's work is praised for its ability to suppress demarcations, arriving thereby at a "multiform and powerful unity" (2:567). This dividing line is breached in the narrator's first reading of Bergotte when he encounters "a hidden stream of harmony, an inner prelude" in what he reads (1:129). Plunging into those images, immersed, all ear, he finds himself falling in love with the author, "a joy that I felt I was experiencing in a deeper, vaster, more integral part of myself from which all obstacles and partitions seemed to have been swept away" (130). The "part" of himself found seems at once whole (integral) and part of an extended, ekphrastic whole. These images for the erotics of aesthetic experience draw on analogies with music and the visual arts as well as nature ("stream" and "swept away" echo in Elstir's work in which air and water dissolve). The "part" realized in language — or, better, in style, stretches back to the immemorial, as Bergotte's language is not current usage nor a matter of conscious life. Much is drawn together by the "thread" he weaves (1:131). Narrative sequence is sacrificed, cut. The reader feels disappointment when it resumes for the joy of reading is found in another text woven at the same time. The access to the real lies in Bergotte's "harmonious," yet "veiled" style, and Elstir's Whistler-like painting answers to these descriptions too. What lies "hidden" nonetheless "explode[s] into [his] consciousness" by way of "imagery" (131), words, in this case drawn from the visual sphere, for what is otherwise wordless.

Introduced to "the gentle Bard" by Odette, "the name Bergotte" makes Proust's narrator "start, like the sound of a revolver" (2:164). Bergotte stands before him "like one of those conjurers whom we see standing whole and unharmed, in their frock coats, in the smoke of a pistol shot out of which a pigeon had just fluttered" (165). The scene of the meeting continues through the imagery, through a series of "likes." Out of the gun aimed "point blank" at the narrator Bergotte emerges in the haze: Shooter and shot change places; the lethal weapon emits a pacific dove and, at the same time, the "godlike elder" (163) the narrator had imagined from reading Bergotte is replaced by "a youngish, uncouth, thickset and myopic little man, with a red nose curled like a snail-shell and a goatee beard" (165). The imagined author has "vanished in the dust of the explosion" leaving behind only his work. In the description of the scene the physically real Bergotte seems less real than the metaphors in which he is inscribed. Revolver dust crosses the two domains as well as the relation between narrator and narration. So, too, upon first reading Bergotte, the narrator had been especially pleased to find his own thoughts had already been written by Bergotte in "mirrors of absolute truth" (1:132) that are those of a conjurer with a magic lantern. Reading Bergotte is a love affair akin to his with Albertine, who emerges from the haze of the gang of girls, or with Gilberte, "a repetition that manages to suggest a fresh truth" (2:648), or like Swann's affair with Odette for that matter, that began on an "aesthetic basis" (1:582).

The narrator's devotion to Bergotte had been consolidated after discovering that Swann knows him, that Gilberte is his constant companion. He falls in love with her thanks to her proximity to Bergotte. Bergotte may descend like a god to raise the narrator by way of his "perfected spirit" (2:132), but the "spirit" — mind, breath, soul — that penetrates the unknown life, the secret life lost in time, is also what the lover seeks in the beloved. He loves Gilberte "on account of all the unknown element[s] in her life in which I longed to be immersed, reincarnated, discarding my own as a thing of no account," and it is because of Bergotte that he "had first loved Gilberte" (1:582). The two loves coincide and reverse like the revolver shot, "now it was above all for Gilberte's sake that I loved him." Who/what is it that he loves?

First meeting Bergotte in person, the Bergotte whom he had "slowly and deliberately elaborated for myself, drop by drop, like a stalactite, out of the transparent beauty of his books, ceased" (2:165). Conjured up by the name Bergotte, perhaps an amalgam of the etymological root *ber-* that in French suggests cradling, being held, and *Gott,* the German word for "god," dispatched by his physiognomy, he is reconstituted by a voice whose monotony and odd inflection create "a plastic beauty independent of whatever his sentence might mean" (2:169), the aesthetic basis upon which Bloch had recommended Bergotte in the first place. In this emulsification language becomes meaningful in its meaninglessness, a "harmonious flow of imagery," to mix metaphors (169), that delivers "a priceless element of truth held in the heart of each thing." This element may be the one sought too in the beloved. Its pricelessness negatively empties the fullness of the thing it is. This is Proust's heart sutra. "Perhaps there exists but a single intelligence of which everyone is a co-tenant, an intelligence toward which each of us from out of his own separate body turns his eye" (2:195). Eve marks this sentence as Plotinian (*Weather in Proust* 2), and remarks how it corresponds to a Buddhist universal permeation and fullness also found in Proust: "Proust has an unusual aptitude ... for replotting linear, genetic, or hierarchic narratives as images, instead, of synchronous profusion and companionship — most especially, self-companionship" (15).

"The priceless element of truth hidden in the heart of each thing" is "the little drop of Bergotte buried in the heart of each thing," a drop "related to all the rest and recognizable, yet ... separate and individual" (2:170). We reach here too the heart of Eve's axiom one. Proust continues, "So it is with all great writers: the beauty of their sentences is as unforeseeable as is that of a woman we have never seen." Seen and unseen meet here, as do the surprise of difference in an elemental sameness of relation.

This element drives Bergotte to his last scene. Just before he dies, he goes to see a painting by Vermeer. A critic has remarked on a "little patch of yellow wall" in the *View of Delft* that Bergotte cannot recall. Dizzy, fixing his gaze, "like a child upon a yellow butterfly that he wants to catch," Bergotte sees how he should have written (5:244), catching at what is fleeting, imperceptible, making it visible. Butterflies, metamorphic, animated creatures that crawl, then fly, intimate material transcendent metamorphoses. This is how the narrator understands Bergotte's realization of the creative life in which one is "obliged to begin over again" (245), to write toward the perfection of a patch of yellow whose representation responds to no social imperative "given sanction in our present life," but awaits "a world actively different from this one" (246) to receive it; an entirely different world, from which we come and to which we return, the narrator posits in a characteristic "as if," that also is in this world, in the art work itself. The life of that work is Bergotte's: "So ... the idea that Bergotte was not dead for ever is by no means improbable" (246). This is not entirely a consolatory realization, as the narrator had found, contemplating his own death "or a survival such as Bergotte used to promise mankind in his books, a survival in which I should not be allowed to take with me my memories, my frailties, my character, which did not easily resign themselves to the idea of ceasing to be, and desired for me neither extinction nor an eternity in which they would have no part" (2:338-39).

Before meeting Bergotte and after hearing from M. de Norpois that he dined with the Swanns, the narrator asks whether Bergotte was there. Norpois responds in a way that anticipates the reception Proust might have feared for the *Recherche,* by reviling Bergotte's "manner" as seductive, precocious, thin, "lacking in virility" (2:61), a trifling without foundation, the embodiment of "Art for Art's" sake. He also deplores Bergotte's irregular sex life. This objection, the narrator, after meeting Bergotte, refuses, seeing his defiance of social convention as making a space for the real life he lives in imagining other lives (2:182).[26] There are two Bergottes, one at home in the social world in which he talks incessantly about his "powerful, rich or noble friends in order to enhance himself" (2:180), though also able to describe Odette as a "whore" to the narrator (199). His real self is the one who writes. It can be attached to a sentence from "The Method of Sainte-Beuve" quoted as Proust's aesthetic credo in the biographical note at the beginning of each volume of the Proust translation I have been citing: "A book is the product of a different self from the one we manifest in our habits, our society, in our vices. If we mean to try to understand this self it is only in our inmost depths, by endeavoring to reconstruct it there, that the quest can be achieved." Hence Eve's "interest in using

---

26 Although Bergotte's sex life is heterosexual it is compared with Charlus's at 4:13-14.

Proust's language and thought as a medium, one with a texture and materiality comparable to other artistic media, that can be manipulated through various processes to show new aspects" (*Weather in Proust* 113). So, string together sentences from Proust across a loom book that manifests depths. Or, take a sentence, for instance, "The most exclusive love for a person is always a love for something else" (2:563), parcel it out, divide it between identical Bodhisattva heads, array word and image across a field half white, half black, so that the heads eventually fade into darkness, deeply veiled. The words stay lit but nonetheless undergo a metamorphosis, from an "exclusive love," supposedly unique and singular, to "a love for something else." Likewise, a person becomes a thing, while the process-in-time becomes an "always" as we read. What persists is the single word "love" doing double duty.

"A Pedagogy of Love"

My heading cites a phrase from the opening section of Lana Lin's "Object-Love in the Later Writings of Eve Kosofsky Sedgwick," chapter two in *Freud's Jaw and Other Lost Objects*. As Lin notes, "love" is a word often coupled with Eve's name, often by those, like her, who never knew Eve. She instances a recent essay by Jonathan A. Allan, who declares his love, and surveys that of others, including some who knew her (like Michael Moon and Jonathan Flatley) and others who did so through her writing. "Love" is the last word in Hawkins's "Re-Creating Eve." Although Katy knew Eve personally, her definition of love points in another direction, to "the depersonalized attention that continually renews our world, inside and out" (280). "Love is the spine, the nexus, that holds together Sedgwick's late work," she continues. That is where we are too, held with her, as she insists in closing sentences that string together a definition of where that is made of a string of "nots" — "not a vase, not a jar, not a body, not a loom or a book or a heart." This holding environment is "nothing that can be contained or created." Lin suggests something similar when she defines Eve's "pedagogy of love" as "reparative work" consisting of "acts of impersonal and anonymous love. Through a generalized care for the world," she continues, "Sedgwick learns to care for herself as an object of love"; "Sedgwick learns how to grasp what sustains her by paradoxically letting go."[27]

"Grasp" is a difficult term here since it seems to give agency to someone who, "paradoxically," is "letting go," not grasping. "Impersonal and anonymous," likewise, when Lin rephrases Eve's care as "generalized," translates the negative/privative "im" and "a" into the inclusive totality of those who have something in common. One key to these difficulties can be found perhaps toward the end of Lin's chapter when she cites Lee Edelman's paradoxical definition of loss: "Loss is what, in the object-relation, it's impossible to lose" (*Sex, or The Unbearable* 47). Loss, Lin glosses, "materializes to fill that gap" (*Freud's Jaw* 109), filling what's lost. Although reparation cannot repair the loss, it does make the need for repair something we all share. Loss becomes something we cannot live without.

Lin's account imagines a time before our loss. Edelman's statement tends in the opposite direction. Loss not only is irreplaceable, it is the condition of our being from the start, or at least once the subject becomes a subject after entering the Lacanian Symbolic. Before that, the phantasmatic Imaginary is a site of wholeness and oneness. Eve's education, and ours through hers in Lin's statements, is a similar temporal process. She loses her breast and realizes her mortality. We had her and then we lost her, entering into the bardo of death-in-life with her. However, in Buddhist teaching, that privileged moment of reality and realization is one we could see anytime. We never were whole, never "had" inherent existence. Lin subtitles her book "Fractured Subjectivity in the Face of Cancer." Does "in the face of" mean before or after cancer? Eve's pedagogy, I venture, is about the time when we are suspended the way her figures in the bardo float.

---

27 Lana Lin, *Freud's Jaw and Other Lost Objects* (New York: Fordham University Press, 2017), 83.

*

Allan formulates his love this way: "One of the things I love most about Sedgwick is that she gives permission to think in different ways, to embrace the challenge of being less paranoid, less anxious, less worried."[28] The challenge of being relieved? Like Lin's, Allan's seems an uplifting project. He writes about the "comfort" he gets from Eve just before the sentence I just quoted. Being "less paranoid, less anxious, less worried" may mitigate Edelman's insistence on paranoid vigilance against false hopes of repair, but it has to be recognized that Eve's pedagogic project was double-edged, less the altruistic self-sacrifice for others that Lin imagines, more an invitation in the direction of Dickinson's recognition that "I'm nobody. … Are you nobody too?" Those lines can seem saccharine and coy, but perhaps are closer to the bracing humor Lin finds in Eve's writing. It's in evidence when Eve asked a reporter in answer to his question about her cancer — whether they "got it all" — "what part of the word 'systemic' don't you understand?" (*Freud's Jaw* 86). Ouch. Zinger.

Eve's pedagogy involved making people smarter, as she and Shannon Van Wey agreed; it can make one smart. It involves recognizing one's stupidity, something that Eve confessed often; the knowingness she fosters lies in the realization that it's not one's own. Lin's love is identificatory; it embraces sameness. Her description of the moment she fell in love with Eve — "this Eve I have never met and yet somehow know and love" (*Freud's Jaw* 114), as she finally and movingly puts it — was ignited by the response to her breast cancer Eve gives in "White Glasses," where she writes, "Shit, I guess I really must be a woman" (*Tendencies* 262). Lin writes, "I had the same reaction Sedgwick had upon reading Silvan Tompkins. I nearly fell out of my chair. As a woman who has never completely identified as a woman per se (or as a man, for that matter), I was both shocked and pleasantly surprised that someone else would have shared my lack of

---

28 Jonathan Allan, "Falling in Love with Eve Kosofsky Sedgwick," *Mosaic* 48, no. 1 (March 2015): 5.

female identification" (*Freud's Jaw* 98). It's hard to say what is "the same" here. Eve's response to cancer is conflated with feelings she and Adam Frank, writing jointly, had, finding themselves found by a text. Lin discovers that Eve shares her own incomplete identification. But is her lack of male identification the same as Eve's identification with gay men? Rather than trying to parse the same by way of a point-by-point correlation, it helps to recall Lin's thesis about part-objects, and the difficulties posed for sameness if no subject is whole to begin with. Did Eve identify as a woman or not? Did cancer make a difference in her identificatory processes? Finally, there is a question of tone — of style — in Eve's response. What is "shit" doing here?

Lin continues her account of how their shared lack of female identification "was the start of an identificatory love with Sedgwick ... only enhanced when I discovered from her husband, Hal, that she and I shared the same oncologist" (*Freud's Jaw* 98). Again, a sharing of the same, "We had undergone some of the most intimate, invasive, and terrifying procedures at the behest of the same doctor." Did they therefore have the same experience? Lin elaborates, by way of a similitude, "It was like finding out we had slept with the same person, or that we had the same mother." How are these discoveries of the same? Indeed, how can likeness explain sameness when "like" means, precisely, like, not the same? Perhaps, for Lin, everything comes to the same thanks to a Freudian, oedipal psychological framework. Can one come to the same by way of difference?

*

How does one fall in love with a writer? Barber and Clark broach this question at the conclusion to "Queer Moments: The Performative Temporalities of Eve Kosofsky Sedgwick," their introduction to *Regarding Sedgwick*. They read Adam Frank and Eve's response to Silvan Tomkins as part of a "melancholically incorporating fantasy" (49), Klein's depressive reparative position. Adam and Eve's advocacy of Tomkins — his bringing them out — entailed, as Barber and Clark stress, the realization of a theoretical moment not their own, not along an identificatory route, almost as an impasse to it. "Like loving, reading extends along so many dimensions that aren't really well described in terms of distinguishing decisively between object-choices, 'this theoretical moment is mine, but *that* one is *hers*,' and so on" (49–50). Barber and Clark sound like Eve here.

"Is it possible to be rescued by a book?" Annamarie Jagose asks, in reference to her own encounter with Eve's writing.[29] It was, she answers, "something like what I imagine it would feel like to be fired from a cannon, spangled and spectacular, newly aerodynamic, holding everything together ... courtesy of an extrinsic propulsive force" (379). It takes Jagose only a few sentences to record her realization that her "likes," her similes, come from Eve's own description of reading Proust. Shot from a cannon, and surviving — how? — by being decimated, liberated, by a force not one's own; the vitality Eve claimed as Craig Owens's.

At the end of "Thinkiest," Jagose attaches her love for Eve with Adam and Eve's for Tomkins. She describes it as a "one-two punch": They love his writing and want us to love it too; they love it because it loves them, and that's why we should too. A "one-two punch" is not exactly a two-way street. It is a knock-out delivered, Jagose suggests, by "stylistic extravagance." Reciprocity crosses itself in a "transferential scene of writing" that Jagose describes as a "gaffe" (381). Their presumption that their being loved makes them lovable to us is a faux pas, a lapse in manners, a breach of the unconscious. Extravagance comes from without — "extra-." It is, to recall Hawkins, "the depersonalized attention that continually renews our world, inside and out" ("Re-Creating Eve" 280). Barbara Johnson called this style "bringing out." Hawkins analogized the process by way of a Zen koan: "To find me, look here. To find me, look elsewhere" — the finger and the moon in Eve's Buddhist pedagogy. Eve describes this as Gary Fisher's style, in that "For all its imposing reserve and however truncated, Gary's is an idiom that longs to traverse

---

29 Annamarie Jagose, "Thinkiest," *PMLA* 125, no. 2 (March 2010): 378.

and be held in the minds of many people who never knew him in another form."[30] A definition of love, re-served, held back, stored for future use; truncated, cut short, cut off, capable of being distributed, disseminated transversely, athwart, aslant, and of being received as being-held. Active-passive change place or occupy the "same" place. Fisher's style is his own idiolect and is, "paradoxically" for "many people" who are like-minded, mindful that a mind "has never been liberated / It has never been deluded / It has never existed / It has never been non-existent." This is as Dudjon Rinpoche puts it in a passage on mind that Eve cites (*Weather in Proust* 209).

*

How to mind Sedgwick might be the pedagogic question that remains. To answer it, I return to Philomina Tsoukala's essay, "Reading 'A Poem Is Being Written': A Tribute to Eve Kosofsky Sedgwick," mentioned earlier. Tsoukala encountered "A Poem is Being Written"[31] at a gathering of lawyers organized by Janet Halley and Jeannie Suk at Harvard in summer 2009. The group met to consider how queer thought about gender might play a role in family law. Among the assigned readings were Eve's essay, which was first published in *Representations* in 1987, as well as the text by Freud that inspired it ("A Child Is Being Beaten"). "Our idea in selecting these two texts was to put the question of masochism directly to the group," Halley writes in her introduction to the issue of *Harvard Journal of Law and Gender* in which some of the papers presented by participants were gathered. From the punishment imagined in Eve's essay, Halley continues, arose "the text, the context, the matrix, the text of her desire to inhabit and transform the power wielded by her parents."[32] Eve's

---

30 Eve Kosofsky Sedgwick, ed., *Gary in Your Pocket: Stories and Notebooks of Gary Fisher* (Durham: Duke University Press, 1996), 291.

31 Eve Kosofsky Sedgwicl, "A Poem is Being Written," *Representations* 17 (Winter 1987): 110–43.

32 Janet Halley, "A Tribute from Legal Studies to Eve Kosofsky Sedgwick: Introduction," *Harvard Journal of Law & Gender* 33, no. 1 (Winter 2010):

insight could reframe family law in its efforts to distinguish a nurturing environment from an abusive one.

Four of the papers pursue these connections. However, Tsoukala chose instead to pay tribute to Eve by describing what reading her "felt like," believing that her "fellow panelists would do a much better job ... linking Sedgwick, Freud, and family law" than she could do. It "felt like Eve Sedgwick had just done something with me or to me" ("Reading *A Poem is Being Written*" 347). It had "the feel of a gradual undoing. ... A hand was coming out of the frame to take away one layer, which then revealed another hand, taking off another layer" (346). She described this experienced as an "unveiling of herself" (346), in which the self in questions was also that of the author. Following Eve's self-exposure, not wanting to "keep her own ass covered" (347), Tsoukala declined to write the expected academic paper. Her experience had been "more like ... a sadomasochistic erotic relationship" of domination and empowerment, "letting me think I had control and then withdrawing it, spanking me and then consoling me." Her response doubles Eve's "visibly chastised" style (*Tendencies* 177). What, finally, did this "obligatory resignification of her violence as love" feel like? "I finished reading the text and it felt like I had just had sex with Eve Kosofsky Sedgwick" ("Reading *A Poem is Being Written*" 347).

Tsoukala recognizes that her itinerary of reading corresponds to the one that Eve imagined, "a fantasy that readers or hearers would be variously — in anger, identification, pleasure, envy, 'permission,' exclusion — stimulated to write accounts 'like' this (whatever that means)" (*Tendencies* 214). "Anger," "Identification," "Pleasure and Envy" head sections of Tsoukala's essay: anger at discipline, being forced to pay attention to Eve's words; identificatory pleasure at feeling that Eve knew her "personally" (she responds by calling Eve "Eve"), coupled with amazement at what treasure lay hidden ("nuggets") in parenthetical throwaways. "Here she was, an author merely three years older than me, who seemed to be years ahead of me in emotional percep-

---

311.

tion and analytical power" ("Reading *A Poem is Being Written*" 343). "Ages ahead," yet always throwing her off by going back again, making undoing the route to progress, like "just when I thought I had a hold on what it was exactly that she was doing, she straddled the paragraph and themes apart, leaving me at the mercy of her (it is now me who can barely stop herself from saying, parental) guidance" (345).

Tsoukala, like Bottom in *A Midsummer Night's Dream,* takes all the positions on offer in Eve's list. "Permission" is in scare quotes as is "like," insisting thereby on the self-difference in the terms themselves. Is permission granted or taken? "Permission" is in doubt because agency is, uncannily, control and letting go. Is "like" a matter of liking or likeness, of sameness, when its possible manifestations include exclusion? This early essay of Eve's — written after *Between Men,* and at an impasse in *The Warm Decembers* and before her work as a queer theorist — anticipates her late work. The enjambment that keeps catching up Tsoukala, pushing her back as she works to go ahead, opens on the possibilities of emptiness. At the end of Eve's essay, and of Tsoukala's as well, Eve comes out as a gay man by claiming a relationship between female anal pleasure (hers, in the dilated sphincter of an essay that keeps letting you in and pushing you out) and gay male sex. Tsoukala has sex with Eve, two women together in the weave created by the huge "empty space" of identification-across that Eve claimed was afforded by the anus (Tsoukala too). Tsoukala writes, "I was titillated and aroused by her discussion of, desire for, and reclaiming of women's anal pleasure" ("Reading *A Poem is Being Written*" 347). They meet, in the productive, creative site of evacuation.

*

The erotic, personal/impersonal space that draws Tsoukala and Eve together has been claimed as public by Melissa Adler. Eve sought to undo the restrictive Library of Congress subject cataloguing of books that, for example, classified *Epistemology of the Closet* as "American fiction — Men authors — History and

Criticism." Thus, her "theoretical positions on the performativity and relations of texts to one another and their readers undergird each chapter" of Adler's book.[33] Eve's remarks on the self-constitutive role of reading in *Tendencies* (4) underlie her project. The library is a site of perversity, she insists in her introduction titled "A Book is Being Catalogued," which riffs on Eve and Freud and quotes from "A Poem is Being Written" where Eve proclaims the library as queer territory, the place that makes her feel "so, simply, *homosexual*." It was there, once she got the hang of the system that occults such knowledge, she found that her "wild guesses" were "almost always right." "If information is being withheld (and to recognize even that is a skill that itself requires, and gets, development)," she writes, "must it not be *this* information?" (*Tendencies* 207).

The library is an erotically charged space, Adler comments, "Some might even regard the pleasurable experiences of browsing and losing and finding oneself in the stacks as an exercise in sadomasochism" (*Cruising the Library* 14). The library seeks to cordon off knowledge into disciplinary categories, but the perverse reader can thread her way through the disciplinary maze at its points of breakdown, re-piecing what has been separated, a reparative project undertaken by the sadomasochistic subject. Adler cites an essay by Donald E. Day that "calls for moving beyond the 'user' as generally conceived by information science toward a conceptualization that views subjects and objects as co-constitutive and co-emergent with 'in-common zones for affects between bodies'" (173). In such a formulation, subjects and objects meet in the "in-common" between, a space in which differences, even those between the living and the dead, cease to matter as such. This is also to say that this nothing that matters is what is.

*

---

33 Melissa Adler, *Cruising the Library: Perversities In the Organization of Knowledge* (New York: Fordham University Press, 2017), xiv.

Arriving here again at questions about likeness and difference, identity and identification. I draw towards a conclusion thanks to work by two former students of Eve's, Jonathan Flatley and José Esteban Muñoz. Flatley's "Unlike Eve" was delivered at the Boston University conference on Halloween 2009. His title reflects a question that he was asked after giving a job talk at Harvard, "What makes you different from Eve Sedgwick."[34] His response was flummoxed since he wanted to answer with "a fierce avowal of my desire to be like Eve" ("Unlike Eve" 229). What he should have said, Eve suggested to him afterwards as they talked about his humiliating experience, was what she would have said in his place, "Unlike Eve Sedgwick, I would take a job at Harvard" (229). There is a dizzying play of saying no and yes here, of likeness and unlikeness at once in Eve's witty, scathing response. These latitudes are crucial in Jonathan Flatley's 2017 book, *Like Andy Warhol,* which emphasizes how likeness, since it does not mean same as, can be a queer route to difference.

One such extension is José's subject in "Race, Sex, and the Incommensurate: Gary Fisher and Eve Kosofsky Sedgwick," republished in *Reading Sedgwick*. It was first published in 2013, the year of his untimely death, and initially delivered at the 2010 MLA convention. He takes off from Eve's fantasy about the reception of "A Poem is Being Written" and allies it to Jean-Luc Nancy's project in *Being Singular Plural* and later work on sense and the commons. "A commons of the incommensurate" found in Nancy is not liberal equivalence which reduces others into the same, a form of domination.[35] Rather, it is an in-commonness made "along relational lines," since that is what we all share. We are all in relation to each other, neither self-constituted, nor self-same. The self-distantiation that, for example, separates Gary Fisher's poetics of racial submission from politics can be put beside the empowerment of Eve's masochistic poetics. Neither

---

34 Jonathan Flatley, "Unlike Eve," *Criticism* 52, no. 2 (Spring 2010): 228.

35 José Estaban Muñoz, "Race, Sex, and the Incommensurate: Gary Fisher and Eve Kosofsky Sedgwick," in *Reading Sedgwick*, ed. Lauren Berlant (Durham: Duke University Press, 2019), 161.

position is a straightforward re-inscription of the identity politics associated with race or gender. Eve and Gary Fisher share an identity in writing that touches on the irreducible plurality that Nancy affirms. Being not-one (nonce) is what each of us has in common. Commonness does not erase difference in finding grounds for likeness. It is a modus vivendi, the route towards "a living in common" ("Race, Sex, and the Incommensurate" 162) in a world we all share differently, differentially, a likeness that could as readily include hating as liking.

"Eve was abundantly and enthusiastically available for various practices of resemblance, identification, and imitation," Jon Flatley concludes the introduction of his essay ("Unlike Eve" 225). Barber and Clark juxtapose Eve's fantasied reception and response to "A Poem" with her announcement of "availability," modeled on Michael Lynch's "availability," in "White Glasses" (*Tendencies* 261). "Being available for identification to friends, but as well to people who don't love one," Eve writes, "even to people who may not like one at all or even wish one well" (cited by Barber and Clark 19). This was her position she affirms as a queer theorist at the opening of "Making Things, Practicing Emptiness," commenting on making herself "available," where she writes, "To be able to fill this role for a while, and substantially affect the shape of some antihomophobic approaches, was a tremendous privilege" (*Weather in Proust* 70).

The meaning of such "availability" is raised by Anne-Lise François in "Late Exercises in Minimal Affirmatives." Her essay about Eve develops from *Open Secrets,* a book that she describes as about nothing, making nothing happen, about minimizing attachment to a world minimally attached to you. Availability to being hated or loved, making oneself — or, better, parts of oneself that do not cohere as one self — available, invites the sharing (out) that José Muñoz explored. In "Queer Patience," Karin Sellberg also invokes Nancy and describes Eve's availability in terms of the "open mesh of possibilities" enunciated in *Tendencies.* Sellberg posits that Eve's readers "become individual little parts of the continually expanding set of relations that is Sedgwick."[36] By "Sedgwick" Sellberg means Eve's writing: "We find one another in the poetic flow of her phrases, words, and inflections" ("Queer Patience" 199). "Her writing," she writes, "is a space that simultaneously opens us up and brings us together" (200).

François links Eve to Roland Barthes and William Empson, joining them in their advocacy of "ease, effortlessness, instaneity, precarity," as they offer themselves up to the transience of existence, to coming as we are.[37] Eastern thought and texts model this availability. Barthes comments that the haiku, which seems at once to bear no meaning and yet is perfectly intelligible word by word, is a way of being available and dispensable — "disposable, serviable," (quoted in "Late Exercises" 39). Availability marks how we are, how Eve offers herself in granting "permission" to let go. François points to the dystopian side of this position especially now in an academy performed by disposable workers or in the deskilling of labor enjoined by superficial (or machine) reading; more specifically in Orientalizing dangers in the critics she compares to each other. However, she concludes, and I with her, that their stepping aside is "not simply a lapse or a checking out" (50). Or, if it is a "checking out" (in another sense of the phrase, attending to), it involves regarding what is when we are not.

---

36 Karin Sellberg, "Queer Patience: Sedgwick's Identity Narratives," in *Reading Sedgwick*, ed. Lauren Berlant (Durham: Duke University Press, 2019), 194.
37 Anne-Lise François, "Late Exercises in Minimal Affirmatives," in *Theory Aside*, eds. Jason Potts and Daniel Stout (Durham: Duke University Press, 2014), 49.

Come As You Are

Eve Kosofsky Sedgwick

Eve delivered this talk at a conference on "Transforming the Culture of Death and Dying In America," organized by the Humanities Institute at SUNY Stony Brook on November 18–19, 1999, and again at the CUNY Graduate Center on March 21, 2000. Melissa Solomon quotes from the copy of the Stony Brook talk that Eve gave her, and which she kindly copied for me as I was preparing the paper for publication, in "Flaming Iguanas, Dalai Pandas, and Other Lesbian Bardos (A few perimeter points)." My copy text was thought to be "the only known ms. of this paper," as David Kosofsky wrote on the copy he sent me on June 28, 2009. I have adopted the fifteen or so small handwritten insertions in it to a text otherwise almost identical to Melissa's copy of the original talk. Both are headed identically, with Eve's full name and "SUNY-SB Conference" below it in the top left corner. The emendations seem likely to have been made for delivery at CUNY. In the opening section, the phrase that reads "that time, by now almost four years ago" originally read "that time, three, by now almost four years ago." The paragraph late in the essay that opens "A few months ago, getting a checkup, I mentioned to my oncologist an academic conference on death and dying," originally read "Last week, getting a checkup, I mentioned this conference to my oncologist." Maggie Nelson reports on the talk and accompanying exhibit in "In the

Bardo with Eve Sedgwick." Nancy K. Miller includes some observations on it in "Reviewing Eve."

I have left stand the capitalization of Eve's title that I changed to more conventional usage in my essay on her, assuming the ontological significance of not capitalizing "you." The notes to the photograph by Joseph Rock and the interview with Rick Fields are in the original manuscript. Eve did not note the source for her quotations from the Heart Sutra. They appear to be based on the translation distributed by the Kuan Um School of Zen founded by Seung Sang in 1983, available on the Providence Zen Center website. It is not identical to the similarly lineated much abbreviated text and commentary of the Mahā Prajñā Heart Sutra in Sang's Compass of Zen.

Come as you Are

Let me start with a word about the slide show, which isn't particularly synchronized with this talk but meant to form a sort of musical background for it. Textiles and Buddhism are two of the main things I'm talking about today, so the slides represent, although sometimes rather loosely, a collection of images of textiles in and around Buddhist culture and practice. Most of the pictures come from five places in Asia: the Kathmandu Valley in Nepal, from central Tibet, from Kyoto, from the Dazu grottoes in Szechuan, or from the old capital at Ayutthaya in Thailand. So they include quite a lot of variety in terms of their Buddhism, in terms of textile craft, and also in terms of representational idiom.

Now, I think many of these images are very beautiful, but if I may ask a rather blunt question, what are these things doing in my *life*? I mean, in *my* life? Why textiles; why Buddhism? I know it's way out of line for a speaker to ask this question, except in a rhetorical way. It's my job to make my topic, whatever it may be, seem so overdetermined as to be entirely inescapable. I'm not supposed to still be wondering, or to admit it if I do wonder. But I do still wonder, and I wondered it even more at the time, three or four years ago, when these two motives, the textiles, the

Buddhism, came bounding into my life. In so many ways, the point of them for me was to be way underdetermined. I think back on that moment a lot — I mean a lot, maybe even compulsively — because it bears so much the stamp of mortality, my mortality. It was the time when I learned that the breast cancer for which I'd been treated half-a-dozen years earlier had silently metastasized to my spine and hence had become incurable.

Actually, it was just before this diagnosis that I was finding that I had fallen suddenly, intrusively, and passionately in love with doing textile work. That is, before the *diagnosis,* but I think it may have happened after I started having the neck pains that were misdiagnosed for several months before they turned out to represent the cancer recurrence. I can't exactly remember the order in which things happened, actually. I just found myself cutting up fabrics to make into other fabrics — appliqués, collages. It was also before the diagnosis, though also I think after the pain started that I found myself reading about Tibetan Buddhism.

When I say this moment bears the stamp of mortality, the image seems to be almost literal. You know how, when you get traumatic or really life-changing news, the people you happen to be with at that moment become special to you just because of being annealed into that instant of time? It's like that. In fact, even to wonder about the Buddhism, the textiles, their conjunction, their sudden and by now very big presence in my life — it could be that the sense of wonder represents a way to let myself keep revisiting that time, by now almost four years ago, when the abstract knowledge of my mortality got so shockingly personal and real. I don't know whether revisiting it so much is more a way of making its realization not real, or more real, to me today.

*

Anybody's engagement with Buddhism, in a culture to which it's so far from native, marks a distinct moment within many diverse histories. For me it was closely linked to this most ordinary and yet oddly privileged of encounters, the tête-à-tête with mortality. Such encounter does involve a privilege, though not an absolute one, with respect to reality. As advertised, it does concentrate the mind wonderfully, even if by shattering it, and makes inescapably vivid in repeated mental shuttle-passes the considerable distance between *knowing* that one will die and *realizing* it. If anything, with all the very exigent lifelong uses that each of us has for the idea of dying, whether shaped by depression, hysteria, hypochondria, existential heroics, coupled with the seemingly absolute inaccessibility of our own death to our living consciousness, death offers in both Western and Buddhist thought the most heightened example of reality, where reality is taken to indicate precisely a gap between knowing something on the one hand, and on the other understanding it as real.

*

Here's a poem I wrote just shortly after that time:

Death

isn't a party you dress up for, man,
it's strictly come-as-you-are, so don't get too
formal, it's useless. Don't grab that prosthesis,
those elevator shoes, or girdle to jam your tummy
in, for your interview with Jesus or
forty-nine days in the bardo of Becoming.
The point's not what becomes you, but what's you.
Why did I buy those silk PJs with feathers
so long before the big affair began?
I've always slept in the nude. Now I sleep in the nude forever.

*

Actually, I've always loved textiles. I used to sew my own clothes, though ineptly, back in college when I had time for it and no money, and the feel of any kind of fiber between my thumb and fingers, in a gesture I probably got from my grandmother who also taught me to crochet and embroider, just is the rub of reality, for me. It's funny that the same brushing-three-fingers gesture is mostly understood to whisper of money, the feel of the coin, as a bottom-line guarantee of reality. I've learned that it's also called "the weaver's handshake," because of the way a fabric person will skip the interpersonal formalities and move directly to a tactile interrogation of what you're wearing.

So, I've always loved textiles, without doing much about it, but something different was happening right around then, something that kept kidnapping me from my teaching and writing tasks and pinning me to my kitchen table with a mushrooming array of "arts and crafts" projects and supplies. Why? Here's one thing that was different: I think I was finally giving up the pretext of self-ornamentation, to which my love of textiles had always clung before. I had all these gorgeous clothes I'd bought but never ever wore. It's funny that it wouldn't happen before age forty-six, or that it *could* happen then, but somehow, I think I got it, that to tie my very acute sense of beauty to the project of making *myself* look beautiful was definitely a mug's game. Apparently, the notion of a visual/tactile beauty that might be impersonal, dislinked from the need to present a first-person self to the world, came as news to me — late, late news. But exciting! My fingers were very hungry to be handling a reality, a beauty, that wasn't myself, wasn't any self, and didn't want to be.

*

There's an enigmatic photograph that seems related to this. Taken in 1926 on the China/Tibet border, by the Viennese-American botanist Joseph Rock, it shows, as the caption explains, "A [Buddhist] monk on the banks of the upper Yellow River [who] repeatedly raises and lowers a[n engraved] board on the surface of the water, each time 'printing' the river with images of Buddhist deities which are carried away downstream."[1]

Of course, the varieties of Buddhist culture contain lots of analogues to this practice. Every time the wind blows, the air of Asia gets "imprinted" by the text of slips of paper tied to trees in Japan, or by chains of prayer flags in Nepal and Tibet. When small handheld prayer wheels get rotated by the flick of a lone pedestrian's wrist, or huge ones by the muscular push of monks or pilgrims, the wheel of Dharma is itself turned.

The prayers on these prayer flags and wheels are pictures and sutras — representing dharma, truth, what is — rather than requests addressed to a powerful being; so what happens here, again, is a promulgation of something, something that simply exists, by no one, to no one. It's in the unanswerable impersonality of practices like these, I think, that one feels the real force of Buddhist atheism. No one sends the message, concomitantly no one receives it, and yet it — what? — it messages, messages itself on the wind and water, always beside the splitting "point" of directional address, in a way that somehow *helps*; if only through its promiscuous, sublime refusal to generate the rhetorical dyad of subject and object, or agent and acted-upon.

*

In *The Tibetan Book of Living and Dying*, Sogyal Rinpoche offers an image that, when I first read it, filled me with a comical sense of recognition:

> Imagine a person who suddenly wakes up in hospital after a road accident to find she is suffering from total amnesia. Outwardly, everything is intact: she has the same face and form, her senses and her mind are there, but she doesn't have any idea or any trace of a memory of who she really is. In

---

[1] Michael Aris, *Lamas, Princes, and Brigands: Joseph Rock's Photographs of the Tibetan Borderlands of China* (New York: China Institute in America, 1992), 86.

exactly the same way, we cannot remember our true identity, our original nature. Frantically, and in real dread, we cast around and improvise another identity, one we clutch onto with all the desperation of someone falling continuously into an abyss. This false and ignorantly assumed identity is "ego."

So, ego, then, is the absence of true knowledge of who we really are, together with its result: a doomed clutching on, at all costs, to a cobbled together and makeshift image of ourselves, an inevitably chameleon charlatan self that keeps changing and has to, to keep alive the fiction of its existence. In Tibetan ego is called *dak dzin,* which means "grasping to a self." … The fact that we need to grasp at all and go on and on grasping shows that in the depths of our being we know that the self does not inherently exist. From this secret, unnerving knowledge spring all our fundamental insecurities and fear.[2]

It's not that I resonated so much with the notion of a true identity hovering somewhere behind the false ones, but it did seem so plausible that one would respond in exactly that way if one somehow did forget just who one was. All the dreams in which I'm sitting on somebody's thesis defense but can't remember ever seeing them before much less reading their dissertation; feel desperate to cover over this gap in my cognitive continuity; and in the event prove able to *do just fine* with it, generating ornery objections, judicious praise, and endlessly articulated opinions with the best of them. Whew! Leaving me to wonder, by the way, in these dreams, whether everybody on the committee might be as clueless as myself. The compulsive way we "argue" by showing each other's opinions to be mutually contradictory, as if we could best conceal the pathetic, makeshift patchiness of our own ego by exposing that of someone else.

Generating opinions, in fact, came to feel like a key to this desperate ego-retro-improvisation, and strikingly so in my academic world — opinions as a way of laboriously, noisily, endless-

---

2   Sogyal Rinpoche, *The Tibetan Book of Living and Dying* (New York: HarperCollins, 2002), 120–21.

ly treading water rather than risk submersion in the salty depths of one's amnesia. One of the reasons I found I loved making *things,* weavings and collages, rather than texts: things neither hold nor are opinions and, ideally, cannot be mistaken for them.

*

What's with the amnesia thing, though? Why identify so strongly with that? I have some ideas, though I'm not quite sure. For one thing, though I didn't exactly find myself in a hospital with no memory of my name, I did suddenly find myself wearing an outer-space-looking neck brace, getting lots of attention from very grave-looking doctors, getting my body "imaged" with a minute intensiveness that descended to the level of cells and molecules, and being gently told to think in terms of maybe two or six more years of life instead of maybe thirty or fifty. I'd already learned from the original cancer diagnosis that a common response to catastrophic news, at any rate one that I seem prone to, is a quite violent pulverizing of the attention span. It's probably a great defense mechanism, a kind of enforced "one day at a time." Sufficient unto this particular second is the disaster thereof, so don't make any connections with the last second or the next. It's an effect that can take a long time to recede — that is, if it ever does. Not so surprising, then, that at that juncture I felt closer to the amnesia than to the project of patching together a coherent story to conceal it.

What may have been adding to that sense of amnesia is the accumulating cognitive effect of the various cancer therapies I underwent. Most of the (little) research on so-called "chemobrain" focuses on high-dose adjuvant chemotherapy, which I didn't have, but it often seems to me that I do feel the accumulated cognitive effects of some combination of the original chemo I took and the subsequent years of radical hormone suppression. I wouldn't say I feel stupider now than before — but I'm encountering a whole lot more verbal blockages, some of them quite dramatic, and as for numbers, the only appropriate phrase is "Forget it." In fact, before I learned about the phenomenon of chemobrain, I often wondered whether I might have suffered one or more small, unremarked strokes.

But then it also seems, and I don't know what the ontological status of this observation can be, but it also seems as though the whole baby boomer generation, or maybe just *everybody* in our culture, is suddenly losing our memory together, or at least becoming obsessed with the specter of such cognitive loss. Don't you think so? It's as though all the amnesiacs in that hospital ward were suddenly trembling on the verge of just not bothering to come up with cover stories at all.

Barbara Herrnstein Smith is fond of the notion of the "senile sublime," as she calls it, and I've always been attracted to it, too. She uses it to describe various more or less intelligible performances by old brilliant people, whether artists, scientists, or intellectuals, where the bare, cold bones of a creative structure seem finally to emerge from what had been the obscuring puppyfat of personableness, timeliness, or sometimes even of coherent sense. Who wouldn't find it magnetic, the idea of emerging into this senile sublime?

*

A lot of what I encountered as "Buddhism" at that time came from a then-recently published semi-bestseller by Sogyal Rinpoche, called *The Tibetan Book of Living and Dying*. Sogyal Rinpoche's book is a highly popularized, at the same time impressively inclusive introduction to Tibetan Buddhism, and it spoke to me at that moment because it's so powerfully organized around exactly the issue of making real the encounter with death. What I found out from it is that the wisdom traditions of Tibetan culture have, if anything, a uniquely detailed focus on the experience of death as a privileged instance of the progress from reality to realization. A privileged instance but not the only one: after-death is one among a group of states, also including meditation, sleep, dreams, and dying itself, that are called *bardos*, gaps or periods in which the possibility of realization is particularly available. *Bar* in Tibetan means "in between," and *do* means "suspended or thrown." As Robert Thurman writes, far from *isolating* such moments the scheme of bardos "is used to create in the practitioner a sense that all moments of existence are 'between' moments, unstable, fluid, and transformable into liberated enlightenment experience."[3] Among these various "betweens," however, it is the one just following death, the bardo of Dharmata, that Thurman translates as the bardo of reality.

According to Sogyal Rinpoche, the bardos represent "moments when the mind is far freer than usual, moments ... which carry a far stronger karmic charge and implication" (110). That implication, however, actually involves the possibility of stepping entirely aside from the forced overdetermination of karmic false identity — which is also to say, from the law of cause and effect — through a very simple achievement of recognition. "The reason why the moment of death is so potent with opportunity is because it is then that the fundamental nature of mind ... will naturally manifest" (110). If at this crucial moment we can recognize the impersonal luminosity of mind, that is, recognize it not only as itself but *as ourselves* and not other than ourselves, then whatever becomes of our energies after death will be entirely freed from the sordid or desperate perseverating traces of other, past *mis*recognitions. That is, the individuating, inexorable, karmic laws of dualistic cause and effect will be transformed into, or simply recognized as, the overarching, radically underdetermining, transpersonal freedom called realization.

*

That gap between knowledge and realization, or between truth and reality: may I give a homely example of what I'm talking about? In the fall of 1998, when I was getting ready for my first trip to Asia, I was especially drawn to the sections in each guidebook that make a stab at filling visitors in on local and regional norms of behavior: don't blow your nose in public, don't wear shoes indoors, bring your own tissue paper into the toilet, don't

---

[3] Robert A.F. Thurman, *The Tibetan Book of the Dead* (New York: Bantam Books, 1994), 34.

hold hands in public *except* with someone of your own sex, walk clockwise around temples and stupas. One instruction that turns up in one guidebook after another is that gifts are supposed to be both proffered and received using both hands. This seemed important to remember, not only because it is true in all three of the countries I was visiting on that trip, but also because, as every source agreed, the giving and receiving of small gifts was going to be the warp and weft of any social interaction. So, I stocked up on theory paperbacks, tins of New York State maple syrup, and baby presents for my new nephew in Seoul, and reminded myself repeatedly that when I handed them over or received gifts in return, I should definitely remember to use both hands.

As it turned out, that trip was wonderful, and soon I was reading guidebooks for a second trip to two other Asian countries. And sure enough, it turned out that in Nepal and Thailand you're also supposed to use both hands for giving and receiving presents. Not a surprise — I already knew this rule well. What did surprise me was to look back suddenly and realize, for the first time, that in all the giving and receiving of gifts during the previous trip, I had in fact not once made the necessary mental connection that would have prompted me to perform those acts using both hands. Not once; and yet in some other register I certainly did and still do know the rule perfectly well, and I had firmly in mind the intent of following it.

It was just that —

It was just that what? I don't know how to explain it. It's just that I'm hardly ever all that self-possessed. But what does that mean? Or maybe it's that handing some particular package to Songmin or Fifi or Jo, in some particular apartment, street, or classroom, isn't easily recognized as "giving a gift" to "someone" in "Asia."

Or maybe it is a memory problem. As I mentioned, I do tend to feel as if my mental filing was all done by some temp who made up a brilliant new system and then quit in a huff without explaining it to anyone else.

I want to say that I knew this rule, but still hadn't realized it — that it hadn't succeeded in becoming real to me, real in the same register as Fifi or as my brother's living room. There's nothing necessarily transcendental about this sense of "realization"; all it would have required was someone to perform the humble, maternal office of saying, "Remember? We talked about this at home. Now, when you hand over this present, what do you do?"

Anyway, that's the only sense in which I can think of reality nowadays: reality not as *what's true* but as *what's realized,* what is or has become real. Where is the gap between knowing something — even knowing it to be true — and realizing it, encountering it as real?

Reality in this sense, as it happens, may be entirely orthogonal to the question of truth. The order of truth, after all, is propositional. The order of reality, on the other hand, while it might include people uttering or thinking propositions, isn't itself propositional. For example, there are many true propositions that would describe the room in which we're meeting this afternoon. Not even an infinite number of such true propositions, however, would exhaust or saturate this space in the order of reality.

Other characteristics that distinguish the order of reality from that of truth: the order of reality is spatial as much as temporal. (Maybe that's what makes real estate, *real* estate.) Reality, unlike truth, tends toward analog as much as or more than digital representation. And correspondingly, unlike truth, reality tends toward the non-dual.

I wonder whether it's because of this tropism toward nonduality that the psychology of realization is so much a specialty of Buddhist thought? Whatever the reason, it does seem remarkable both how much attention Buddhism pays to the gap between knowing and realizing, and retroactively, how little attention is paid to it in Western thought. To practice Buddhism, after all, is to spend all the time you can in the attempt to realize a set of understandings most of whose propositional contents are familiar to you from the beginning of your practice. The very existence, the multiplicity, the intensiveness of different

Buddhist traditions testify to the centrality of the project of realization; to the sense of how normal it is for realization to lag behind knowledge by months or eons; and to a concern that any pedagogy of realization is likely to be a hit-or-miss matter haplessly dependent on the contingencies of the individual.

The guidance offered to the newly dead in the *Bardo Thodol* or so-called *Tibetan Book of the Dead,* meant to be read aloud to those undergoing the bardo of reality, has very much the homely, practical structure of that maternal adjuration to "remember, this is what we talked about at home." The main thing needed by the dead, in the Bardo of Reality, is orientation amid the lightshows and ostentatious projections of an anxious, dissolving identity. In Thurman's translation, for instance, on the fourth day in this Bardo, the person is reminded,

> On this fourth day, the red light that is the purity of the element fire dawns. ...Do not fear it! ... you want to flee it .... But ... you must fearlessly recognize that brilliant red, piercing, dazzling clear light as [your own] wisdom. Upon it place your mind, relaxing your awareness in the experience of nothing more to do. ... If you can recognize it as the natural energy of your own awareness, without feeling faith, without making prayers, you will dissolve indivisibly with all the images and light rays and you will become a Buddha. If you do not recognize it as the natural energy of your own awareness, then pray and hold [onto] your aspirations for it, thinking, "It is the light ray of the compassion of the Lord Amitabha! I take refuge in it!" (138–39).

In the *Bardo Thodol,* each day's coaching ends with an encouraging note to the reader-aloud, such as, "When you thus repeatedly orient the deceased, however feeble his affinity, if he does not recognize one wisdom, he will recognize another. It is impossible not to be liberated" (141). As the next day dawns, though, the text resumes wearily but patiently. "However, even though you orient the deceased repeatedly in this way, still through long association with the myriad instincts, and little previous experience with the purified perception of wisdom, even though he is clearly oriented, he is pulled beyond these recognitions by [the deforming traces of cause-and-effect]" (141). So today's apparition is ...

*

Hoping to enable an end-run around this laborious process, in his book, Sogyal Rinpoche details several versions of a visualization practice called *phowa* which, if performed at the moment of death, is supposed to make enlightened recognition possible in the Bardo of becoming. "In fact," he writes,

> you should be so familiar with the practice ... that it becomes a natural reflex, your second nature. If you have seen the film *Gandhi,* you will know that when he was shot, his immediate response was to call out: "Ram ... Ram!" which is, in the Hindu tradition, the sacred name of God. Remember that we never know how we will die, or if we will be given the time to recall any kind of practice at all. What time will we have, for example, if we smash our car into a truck at 100 mph on the freeway? There won't be a second then to think about how to do [the practice], or to check the instructions in this book. Either we are familiar with [it] or we are not. There is a simple way to gauge this: just look at your reactions when you are in a critical situation or in a moment of crisis, such as an earthquake, or a nightmare. Do you respond with the practice or don't you? And if you do, how stable and confident is your practice?
>
> I remember a student of mine in America who went out riding one day. The horse threw her; her foot got stuck in the stirrup, and she was dragged along the ground. Her mind went blank. She tried desperately to recall some practice, but nothing at all would come. She grew terrified. What was good about that terror was that it made her realize that her practice had to become her second nature. This was the lesson she had to learn; it is the lesson, in fact, we all have to

learn. Practice ... as intensively as you can, until you can be sure you will react with it to any unforseen event. This will make certain that whenever death comes, you will be as ready as you can be. (221)

"The point's not what becomes you, but what's you." I realize that in one sense, this kind of exhortation could come straight out of the most vindictive of the Puritan homiletics meant for terrorizing children. And at the moment of my sudden rediagnosis, I was certainly vulnerable to being terrorized in such a way. In fact, I was finding, to my astonishment, that not even a life history as a totally nonreligious Jew was protecting me from getting spooked by middle-of-the-night images of dying and landing in, of all places, hell. I mean, Jews don't believe in hell, but then Jews don't believe in a lot of things that turn out to be real, like Richard Nixon. But while neither atheism nor Judaism seemed to offer protection from such punishing images, my relief came, instead, from two other aspects of the Buddhist thought to which I was getting exposed. First, there were some reflections on reincarnation, which I unfortunately haven't time to discuss here; but second, there was the blessed and welcoming, however cool and impersonal, or, rather, even because of those traits, Buddhist embrace of nondualism. For instance, in the Heart Sutra:

> No ignorance and also no extinction of it,
> and so forth until no old age and death
> and also no extinction of them.
> No suffering, no origination,
> no stopping, no path, no cognition,
> also no attainment with nothing to attain.

In Christianity, by contrast, the notion of getting saved depends on an act of specifically unearned divine grace, in the context of a radically dualistic hypostatization of agency between active and passive. Even under the most immediate stress of mortality, there was just no way I could make sense of or identify with that absolute kind of psychological splitting: it wasn't me. Far indeed from the nondualistic Buddhist realization of the nature of mind, where, in the words of Dudjom Rinpoche,

> Samsara does not make it worse
> Nirvana does not make it better ...
> It has never been liberated
> It has never been deluded
> It has never existed
> It has never been nonexistent.
>
> (*Tibetan Book of Living and Dying* 50)

*

Somewhere in the background of this talk is a project I've had in mind for a while now, a still unrealized project for a conference or an anthology whose title would be something like "Critical Theory, Buddhist Practice." I thought of the project as a way of marking and trying to understand the successive discovery that one after another of the intellectuals my age or younger whom I'm really interested in these days turn out also, on acquaintance, to be at some stage, whether early or advanced, in an exploration of some form of Buddhist practice or thought. I'm not just talking about dying people or Californians here, either. These recognitions have been taking place in the Bible-thumpin' south, the windy heartlands, the Manhattan cosmopole, and the Puritan fastness of New England, as well.

I've no doubt there's a *lot* to be said and thought about such encounters, both as they reflect a zeitgeist or two (or twenty) and as they intertwine with the intellectual, emotional, and spiritual destinies of a lot of really interesting individuals. Among the stories that await more telling, some of the historical ones involve American orientalism of the nineteenth and twentieth centuries, the afterglow of a 1960s counterculture and the deep political discouragement of its cooptation, the longer reverberations of a Beat fascination with Japanese Zen, the fatuities and promiscuities of New Age marketing, the diasporic imperative impelled by the post-1959 shattering of traditional, feudal Tibetan culture, and the funny mix of humility with nativist triumphalism in the rapid emergence of something that nowadays gets called "American Buddhism," though it has barely a nominal relation to anything practiced in the Chinatowns and other Asian immigrant communities scattered broadcast over the map of the United States. In fact Rick Fields, the most loving and critical historian of this movement so far, pointedly denominates it "white Buddhism."

Another set of stories might involve both the aptitudes and the impasses of the critical theory that has shaped these two generations of US academic critics. Aspects of Buddhist thought that initially seem counterintuitive to many people—its rigorous nondualism, for an obvious example, or its sense that individual identity is a delusion as well as a snare—can seem already self-evident and invitingly haimish to anyone whose mother's milk has been deconstruction or, say, systems theory. Furthermore, I think many intellectuals experience a tremendous, grateful relief at encountering a deep, ramified, already long-existent history of treating these shared nondualistic understandings as more or other than a series of propositions to be demonstrated and textual readings to be performed. In some ways it's probably misleading to think of Buddhism as a religion; yet, as with a religion, the distinctive bonds between Buddhism and the question of reality seem to cluster around the issue of practice rather than of epistemology.

The only widespread Western practices I can think of that are even analogous to this occur in evangelical Christianity—the sometimes protracted struggle to be or to understand oneself as saved—or in psychoanalysis. These Western instances are analogous in that both of them frame realization, unlike knowledge, in terms of practices, practices that take place over time. But in psychoanalysis there is still, very often, at least the pretext that progress within analysis equals the achievement of new levels of propositional knowledge, for instance about one's personal history. And meanwhile, the popularity of psychoanalysis within critical theory as a system or a language always tends toward short-circuiting its realization as practice. So, its insights get added in turn to the list of *things to know* rather than becoming manifest as a *way of knowing,* never mind of doing or of being. And yet for many intellectuals, the most efficacious surprise for us in our real encounters with psychotherapy is how little our quickness of apprehension may have to do with the far statelier pace of realization and change. A humbling thing to catch on to, but only so long as one maintains the intellectual's hair-trigger, disavowing contempt for the process of realization in all its real, obscure temporality. Perhaps the most change can happen when that contempt changes to respect, a respect for the very ordinariness of the opacities between knowing and realizing.

In fact I've been struck by the relative impoverishment of any western psychology of knowledge and realization, whether empiricist *or* postmodern, compared with its density and richness in Buddhist thought. If anything, within the framework of the Buddhist respect for realization as both process and practice, the stuttering, exclusive perseveration of epistemological propositions in contemporary critical theory reads as a stubborn hysterical defense. Whether it comes in the form of antiessentialist hypervigilance or, say, of the moralizing Marxist insistence that someone else is evading a true recognition of materiality, all this epistemological fixation, with all its paralyzing scruples or noisy, accusatory projections, can also seem like a hallucinatorily elaborated, long-term refusal to enter into realization as into a complex practice. Rather it can't stop claiming mastery of reality as the flat, propositional object of a single verb, shivering in its threadbare near-transparency: the almost fatally thin "to know."

*

I suppose the contradiction that might be going on with my current practice is then, Why the object fixation onto fiber art *as real*? Forget underdetermination; what can the sublimity of forgetting have to do with the apparent hyper-retentiveness of these "shmatta studies"? What could represent "clinging" to identity more regressively than their collaged evocation of, for instance, the tattered security blanket of babyhood, whose binding I fingered and fingered into filthy rags that I refused to surrender even to be washed?

In my shrink's notes from when I started making these textile collages, he jotted the following from my maunderings on the subject:

SILK WORK — TURNING FABRIC INTO OTHER FABRIC / CHILDHOOD BLANKET WITH THE SATIN BINDING / SKIN HUNGER / ... BRO'S PILLOW 'PIFFO,' HIS DROOLING, "MAKING FISHES" ON IT / MAY SAY SOMETHING ABOUT HOW HUNGRY OUR SKIN WAS FOR TOUCH, BUT ALSO ABOUT OUR HAVING THE PERMISSION TO DEVELOP AUTONOMOUS RESOURCES / ... / TREASURE SCRAPS OF SILK / SOMEHOW THE SILK AND SHIT GO TOGETHER — THE WASTE PRODUCTS, FANTASIES OF SELF SUFFICIENCY, NOT DEPENDENT, SPINNING STRAW INTO GOLD.
(*A Dialogue on Love* 206)

What if, instead of getting scared off by the notion of regression, we could acknowledge that the work of the security blanket, the "transitional object" in Winnicott's phrase, really is continuous with that of the fiber art? Why would it be a scandal if the tasks of dying and those of toddlerhood, such as individuation and even toilet training, were not so different? were, so to speak, molded of the same odorous, biomorphic clay?

Suppose that getting toilet trained is about learning, forcibly, to change the process of one's person into a residual product — into something that instead exemplifies the *im*personal in its lumpishly ultimate and taboo form. Isn't this one of the tasks of dying as well? Suppose the many, stubborn, transformational negotiations with chosen cloth objects at that period are a medium for experimenting with the dimensions and new possibilities of this unwelcome imperative. Another such imperative is the letting go of the infantile cutaneous touch of the person you love, who also loves you. These are also among the tasks of dying.

The Heart Sutra, from which I've already quoted, places at the very head of its undoings of dualism this famous one:

> Form does not differ from emptiness,
> emptiness does not differ from form.
> That which is form is emptiness,
> that which is emptiness form.

Teachings on this sutra emphasize that "emptiness" here, or indeed emptiness anywhere, should be thought of as like the empty space on the inside of a bell; emptiness not blank but vibrant and gravid with subtle energy, potential, and arising. But maybe we can also think of the experimentally fantasied "emptiness" of a child's voided insides, as the child learns to link that to the power of material formation, of the formal and of what is not herself.

*

I've mentioned Rick Fields, the influential American historian and practitioner of Buddhism. Last June, Rick Fields died of cancer at the age of fifty-seven. In an obituary in *Tricycle* magazine, the magazine's editor Helen Tworkov, wrote,

> I saw Rick at his house the Thursday before he died. His skin was sallow and buttery soft, his eyes luminescent. With scratchy, slurred words, he explained that he was feeling woozy. ... Then came a moment when we were alone. In a clear voice suddenly delivered of static, he spoke of the interview that we had done for Tricycle [two years before]. "Do you remember when you said to me," recalled Rick, "you're dying and I'm dying. And you have cancer and I don't. Is there a difference?" Then he continued, trying once more in this lifetime, to help me get it right. "Well, one way of understanding that difference, is that I'm in the bardo of dying and you're not."

A few months earlier Rick had written [on] "The Bardo of Dying' in his journal. ... The bardo of dying begins when you are diagnosed with an incurable illness [and ends only when you enter the bardo of after-death]. Rick had come across these same teachings many times, but he wrote that this time, they "clearly revealed where I am, where I live in the cycle of existence — the endless wheel of life and death. ... To realize this replaces ignorance with knowledge, perhaps even wisdom, or its beginning at least. Ah, *this* is where I am."[4]

It's interesting that Fields hadn't found much to read about this particular bardo. I suppose it's only recently that the bardo of dying, as opposed to that of after-death, has become for many people a sufficiently extensive space to invite a lot of elaboration. Or political éclat (think how much the impact of early AIDS activism came from the stunning novelty of seeing young adults with a fatal disease who were nonetheless physically strong enough, and for a long enough time, to undertake the project of their own, forceful representation). AIDS and cancer are among the grave diseases where, in the absence of cure, modern medicine has offered ever-earlier diagnosis along with, at least for AIDS, delayed mortality. Whether it be through early diagnosis or more effective treatment, at any rate, the bardo of dying has expanded for many of us to a period that can encompass several years or even, sometimes, many. Tworkov remarks that Rick Fields valued "the companionship of those who inhabit the same bardo," a companionship that can even generate a new kind of public sphere, as in the case of AIDS and increasingly, I hope, of people with advanced cancer. These may be years of good health or ill health, of pain or its relative absence, of lassitude or energy. More likely all these are mixed together unpredictably, intermittently, though on a worsening trajectory.

A few months ago, getting a checkup, I mentioned to my oncologist an academic conference on death and dying and remarked that, as far as I could tell from the program, I was the

---

4 Helen Tworkov, "Obituary for Rick Fields," *Tricycle* 9, no. 1 (Fall 1999): 23.

only sick person involved in it. He said, "You know, it's a nice philosophical question at this point, in exactly what sense you can be said to *be* sick." He meant his comment to be cheering, and it actually was — I'm feeling very well, and I liked his acknowledging that.

At the same time, what's harder to explain is the sense of recognition that comes, as Fields put it, with being able to see and say, "Ah, *this* is where I am" — in this bardo, the one of dying. Fields also noted how others, such as the healthy, who "live in different bardos, move perhaps at different speeds, perceive, think, feel perhaps at different frequencies." To say that there seem to be distinctive psychological and spiritual tasks to accomplish in the bardo of dying, for anyone lucky enough to be able to focus and be present to them, is only another way of saying that there are special freedoms to be claimed here: freedoms both of meaning, relation, and memory, yet also from them.

*

When Sherwin Nuland, the physician author of *How We Die,* writes about the way metastatic cancer behaves in the human body, he does so in a chapter entitled, not "The Malignancy," but rather "The *Malevolence* of Cancer" (my emphasis). It's clear that he simply disapproves of such behavior, essentially on civic grounds. Cancer cells, he points out, reproduce promiscuously while they are still immature, becoming drains on society.

> Cancer cells are fixed at an age where they are still too young to have learned the rules of the society in which they live. As with so many immature individuals of all living kinds, everything they do is excessive and uncoordinated with the needs of constraints of their neighbors. ... Malignant cells concentrate their energies on reproduction rather than in partaking in the missions a tissue must carry out in order for the life of the organism to go on. The bastard offspring of their hyperactive (albeit asexual) fornicating are without the resources

to do anything but cause trouble and burden the hardworking community around them.[5]

The 1980s and '90s image of the demonized welfare mother and her terrorizing brood, as sinister as Milton's Sin and Death, is all but explicit; he even refers to the tumor cells' rapacious behavior as "wilding" (208). And however immature, they deserve to be tried as adults. "A cluster of malignant cells is a disorganized autonomous mob of maladjusted adolescents .... If we cannot help its members grow up, anything we can do to arrest them, remove them from our midst, or induce their demise — anything that accomplishes one of those aims — is praiseworthy" (210).

Setting aside the phobic and, still more, the firmly anthropomorphic nature of this language, it's true that the progress of this disease is extremely unpredictable and antinomian. Each type of metastatic cancer has particular sites that it's most prone to seeking out and devouring, in no particular order — breast cancer, for instance, besides often going to bone, has a tropism toward liver, lungs, eyes, brains — but there is no organ, vital or vestigial, including the little toe and the heart, where it won't take hold if the tide of contingency and sheer *un*organization drops it there. The disease's course depends much on the thinnest fabric of whimsy, and not at all on any law — except for the one law, of being fatal.

It's thus that a certain Buddhist problematic becomes so heartfelt in the face of advanced cancer: the coming to terms, and ideally terms of love *if not* of dignity, with a process where endless underdetermination continues to arise and arise in the face of one single overdetermination, whose narrative coherence will be only retrospective. "The point's not what becomes you, but what's you" — if one isn't going to cling desperately to a self, however, another point might be to become *it*; to identify with the fabric and structure of this discohesive fate itself.

---

5 Sherwin B. Nuland, *How We Die: Reflections on Life's Final Chapter* (New York: Vintage Books, 1995), 209.

*

I'll end with one more poem — this one's about toilet training, but it also quotes from the Heart Sutra.

Bathroom Song

I was only one year old;
I could tinkle in the loo,
such was my precocity.
Letting go of Number Two
in my potty, not pyjama,
was a wee bit more forbidding
— and I feared the ravening flush.
So my clever folks appealed
to my generosity:
"What a masterpiece, Evita!
Look! We'll send it off to Grandma!"

Under the river, under the woods,
off to Brooklyn and the breathing
cavern of Mnemosyne
from the fleshpotties of Dayton —
what could be more kind or lucky?

From the issue of my bowels
straight to God's ear — or to Frieda's,
to the presence of my Grandma,
to the anxious chuckling
of her flushed and handsome face
that was so much like my daddy's,
to her agitated jowls,
Off! Away! To Grandma's place!

As, in Sanskrit, who should say
of the clinging scenes of karma,
"Gaté, gaté, paragaté"

(gone, gone, forever gone),
"parasamgaté; bodhi; svaha!"
(utterly gone — enlightenment —
svaha! Whatever svaha means),
Send the sucker off to Grandma.
Gaté, gaté, paragaté;
parasamgaté; bodhi; svaha!

* * *

Floating Columns / In the Bardo

"Floating Columns/ In the Bardo" was the title of the show of Eve's fiber art at State University of New York Stony Brook's Union Gallery in fall 1999 ("Floating Columns" titled an exhibition at Rhode Island School of Design that fall and at the Cedar Creek Gallery in Durham, North Carolina, in spring 2000). For the City University of New York exhibition (in a lounge also used for lectures) the show's title was truncated to "In the Bardo." Eve composed a statement about the original show and revised it slightly for the second occasion. Melissa Solomon provided me with a copy of the original; Hal Sedgwick, responsible for the photos I reproduce, included one that showed the revised statement. It is my copy text. I have left in brackets part of the original title and some wording at the end of Eve's statement in which she furthers a comparison between her earlier and later work. Jason Edwards offers some hypotheses about the exhibition in "For Beauty Is a Series of Hypotheses? Sedgwick as Fiber Artist," a discussion expanded in a forthcoming monograph that he gave me the chance to read. In it he also details the "Floating Columns" show of ten pieces of fabric art displayed on the gallery walls.

A writer and literary critic, I'm largely self-taught as a fiber artist. Despite a lifelong textile obsession, I began this work in earnest only three years ago, around the time I learned that a previously treated breast cancer had become incurable, and also around the time when I became very interested in Buddhist thought.

Tibetan Buddhism has had a strong influence on recent US thought about death and dying largely through such books as Sogyal Rinpoche's popular *Tibetan Book of Living and Dying* based on the so-called *Tibetan Book of the Dead,* an oral reading that offers the recently departed soul a guide through the "bardo" or between-state that immediately follows death. (Tibetan *bar* = in between, *do* = suspended, thrown.) In this bardo, the soul encounters a succession of distracting, often terrifying lights, winds, sounds, and peaceful or even wrathful apparitions of deities. The task and great opportunity of the soul — its way to enlightenment and away from constant rebirth into pain and delusion — is just to recognize these alien manifestations as not other than itself, not other than its own, radiantly sustained awareness. Such a recognition is an entirely simple but apparently, usually impossible one.

As Sogyal Rinpoche points out, "The word 'bardo' is commonly used to denote the intermediate state between death and rebirth, but in reality bardos are occurring continuously throughout both life and death," and because of their threshold nature "are junctures when the possibility of liberation, or enlightenment, is heightened." Among the bardos specifically identified in Tibetan Buddhism are those of rebirth, living, falling asleep, dreaming, and "the painful bardo of dying," which occupies the space between contracting a terminal illness and death itself. With certain illnesses (cancer and HIV, for instance) and in the present state of medicine, that transitive suspension or gap, the bardo of dying, may be quite an extended one. Like other bardos, it is electric with spiritual possibility as well as with pain and loss.

The present installation offers a certain experience of the bardo of dying. The large (my size), light figures, analogous to the peaceful and wrathful deities of that other bardo, are bearers of some crucial aspects of this experience, holding them open to such psychic operations as identification, disavowal, projection, recognition, rage, or reparation. The figures' strongest representational ties are to the disorienting and radically denuding bodily sense generated by medical imaging processes and illness itself, on the one hand, and, on the other, to material urges to dress, to ornament, to mend, to re-cover and heal. Correspondingly, a central element of each figure is the vertebral column, which I daily experience as both physically disintegrating, yet still offering a pathway for vital energy and buoyancy. These are not opposites: in different ways, both cancer and Buddhism highlight the need of coming to loving terms with what's transitory, mutable, even quite exposed and ruined, while growing better attuned to continuities of energy, idiom, and soul.

The sustained encounter with mortality is tied not only to a sense of sublimity and abstraction but also to a great appreciation for the quotidian sensuousness of fiber materials and processes. As a writer exploring the fields of gay/lesbian studies and queer theory, I've long gravitated toward nondualistic approaches to ideas and genres [– working, for example, at the boundaries between poetry and prose, between activism and scholarship]. The pieces in this show also mean to span such productive, highly charged, and permeable boundaries as those between craft and art; between woven fiber (cloth) and nonwoven (paper, felt, soie mariée); between feeling and meditation, or gravity and lightness; at last, between making and unmaking.

COME AS YOU ARE

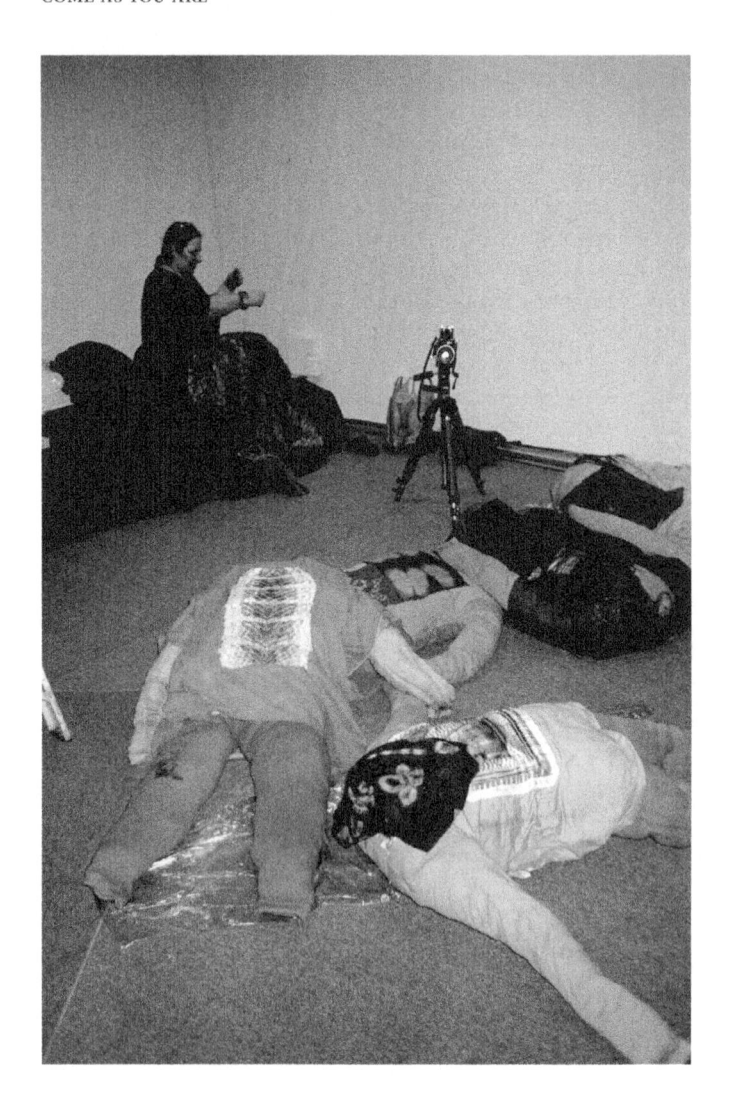

COME AS YOU ARE

COME AS YOU ARE

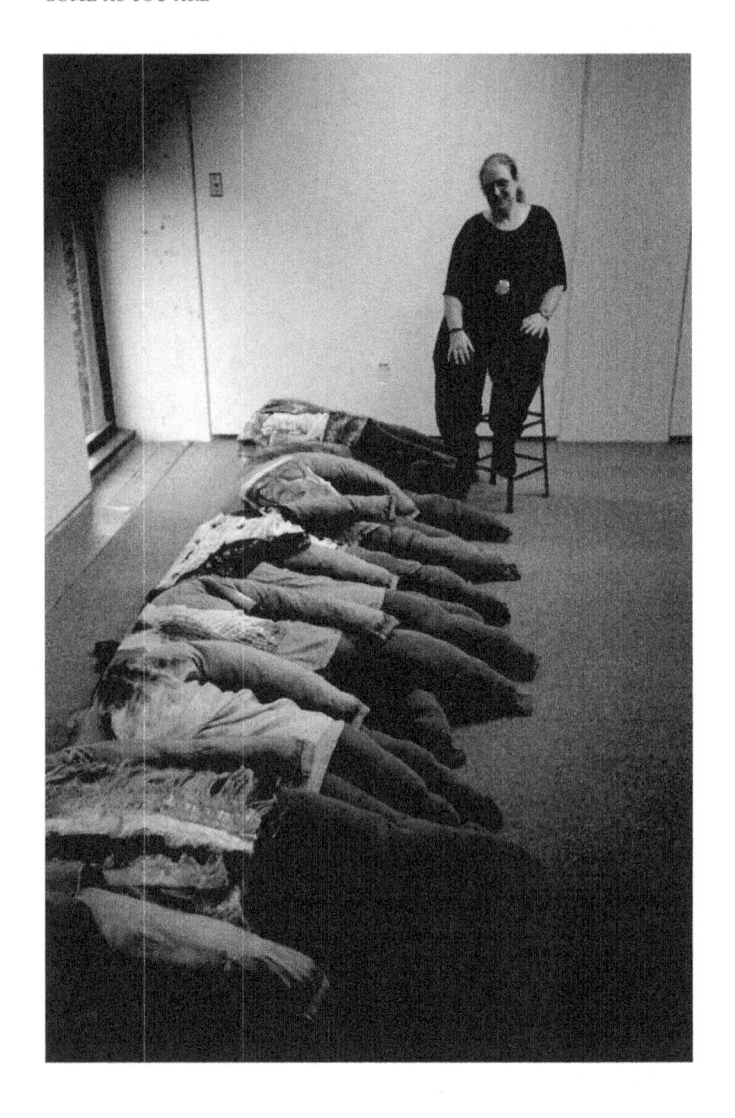

COME AS YOU ARE

COME AS YOU ARE

COME AS YOU ARE

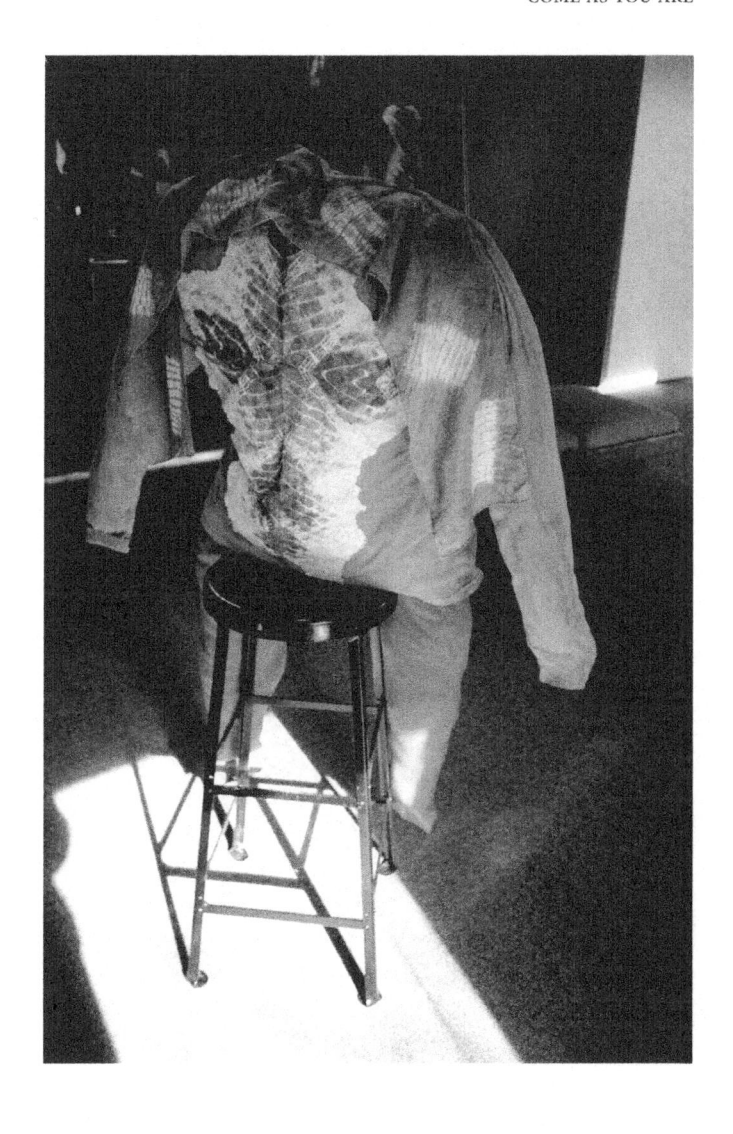

COME AS YOU ARE

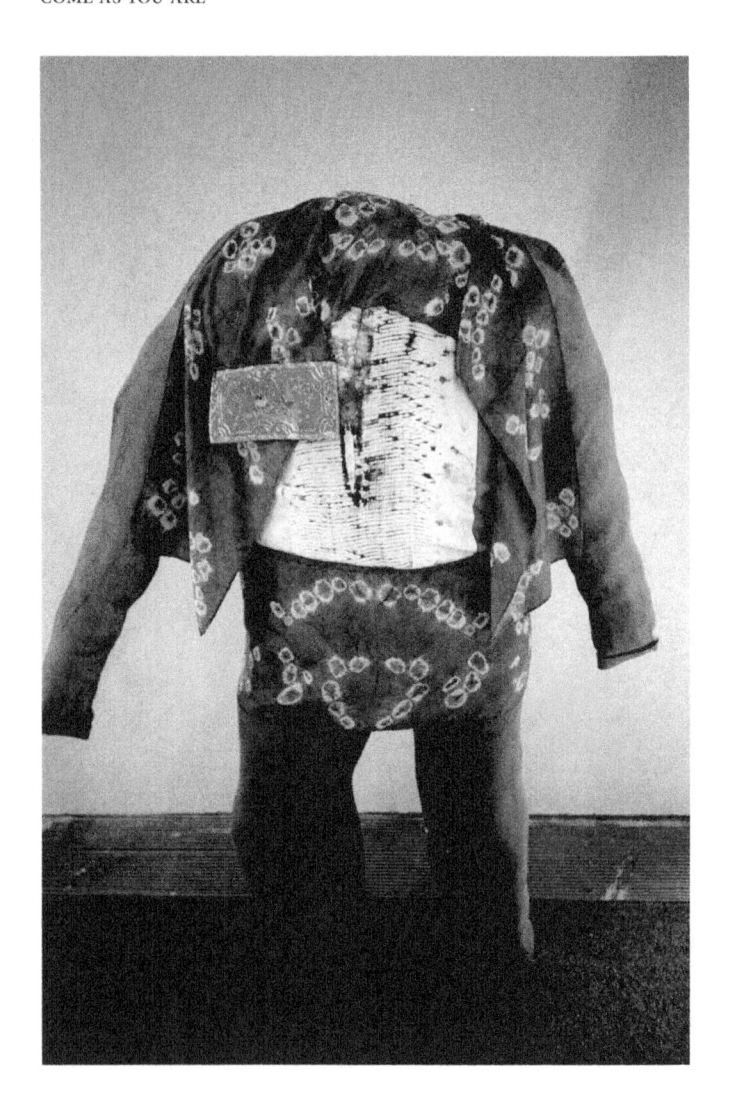

COME AS YOU ARE

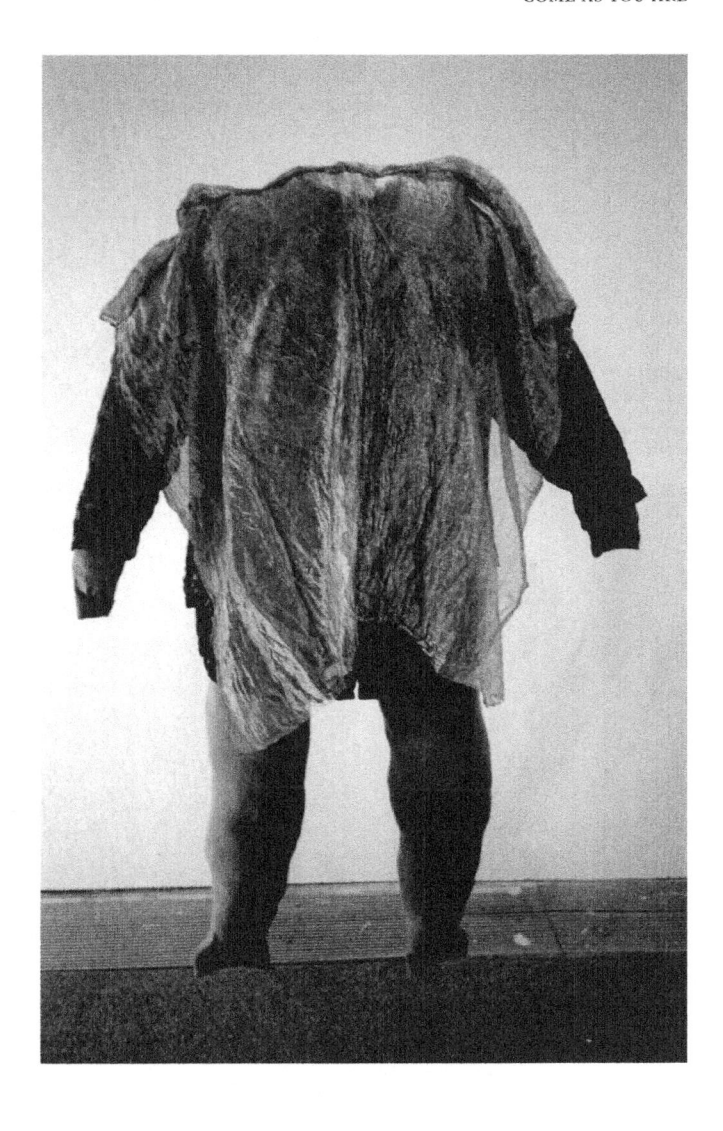

COME AS YOU ARE

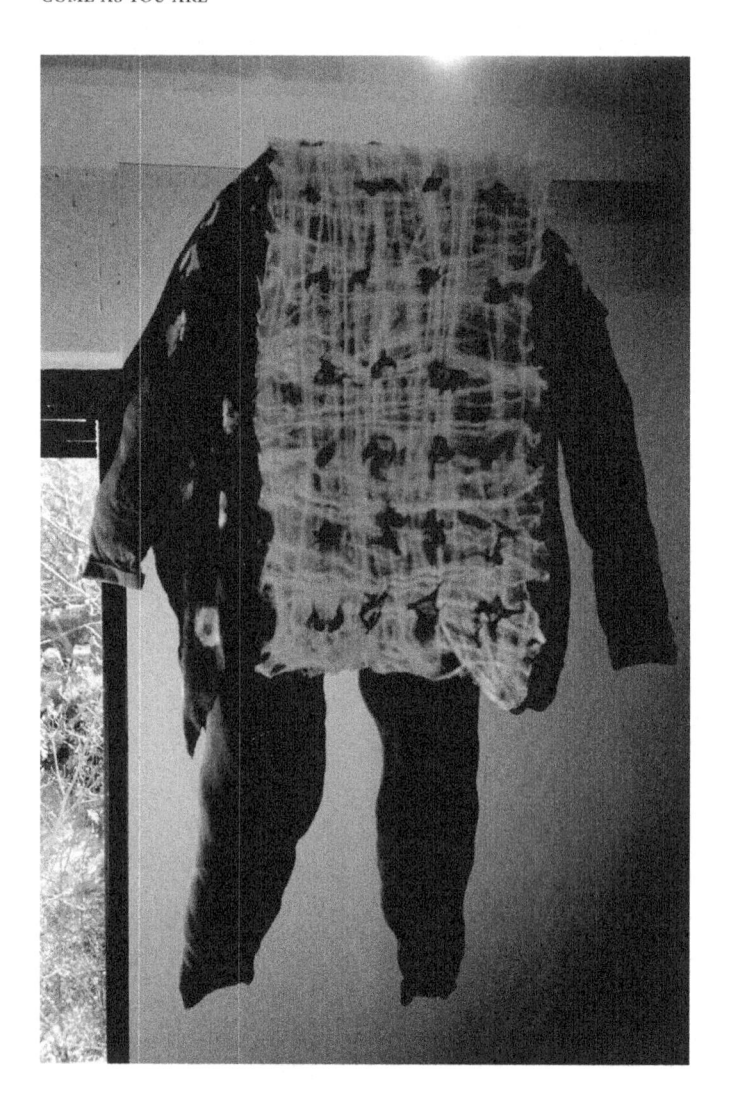

COME AS YOU ARE

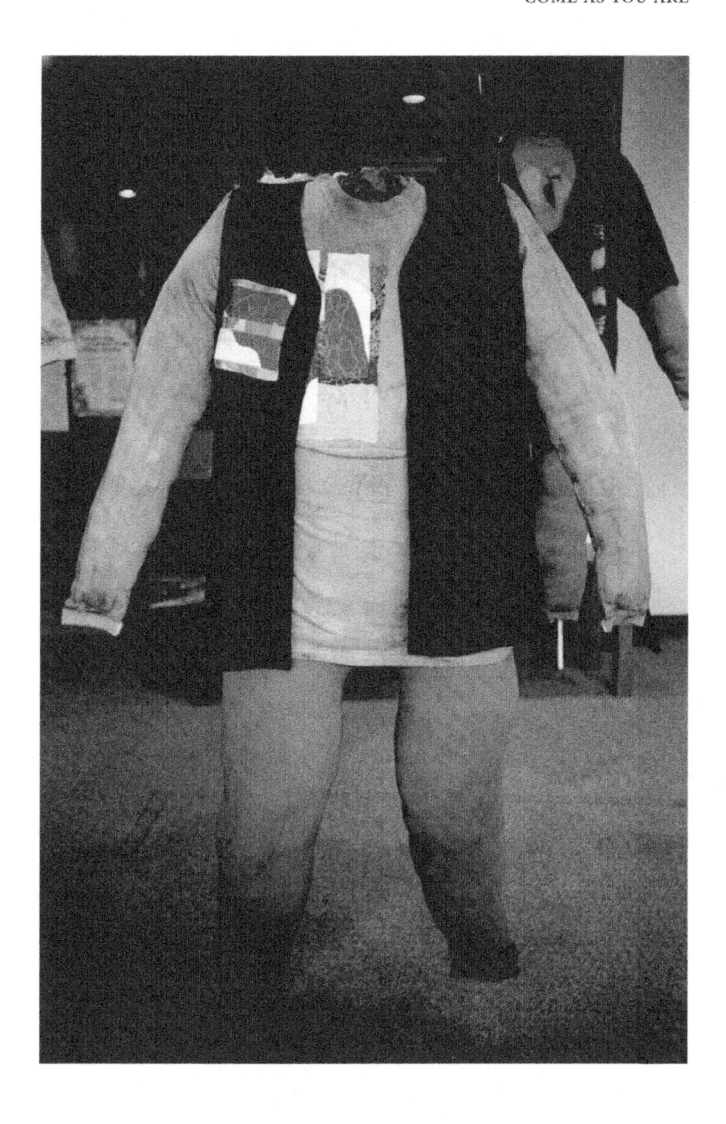

COME AS YOU ARE

COME AS YOU ARE

COME AS YOU ARE

Works Cited

Adler, Melissa. *Cruising the Library: Perversities in the Organization of Knowledge.* New York: Fordham University Press, 2017.

Allan, Jonathan A. "Falling in Love with Eve Kosofsky Sedgwick." *Mosaic* 48, no. 1 (March 2015): 1–16. DOI: 10.1353/mos.2015.0010.

Aris, Michael, and Patrick Booz. *Lamas, Princes, and Brigands: Joseph Rock's Photographs of the Tibetan Borderlands of China.* New York: China Institute in America, 1992.

Barber Stephen M., and David L. Clark. "This Piercing Bouquet: An Interview with Eve Kosofsky Sedgwick." In *Regarding Sedgwick: Essays on Queer Culture and Critical Theory,* edited by Stephen M. Barber and David L. Clark, 243–62. New York: Routledge, 2002.

Berlant, Lauren. "Eve Sedgwick, Once More." *Critical Inquiry* 35, no. 4 (Summer 2009): 1089–91. DOI: 10.1086/605402.

———. "Reading Sedgwick, Then and Now." In *Reading Sedgwick,* edited by Lauren Berlant, 1–5. Durham: Duke University Press, 2019.

———. "Two Girls, Fat and Thin." In *Regarding Sedgwick: Essays on Queer Culture and Critical Theory,* edited by Stephen M. Barber and David L. Clark, 243–62. New York: Routledge, 2002.

Berlant, Lauren, and Lee Edelman. *Sex, Or the Unbearable.* Durham: Duke University Press, 2013.

Bohm, David. *Wholeness and the Implicate Order.* London: Routledge, 1980.

Butler, Judith. "Capacity." In *Regarding Sedgwick: Essays on Queer Culture and Critical Theory,* edited by Stephen M. Barber and David L. Clark, 109–19. New York: Routledge, 2002.

———. "Proust at the End." In *Reading Sedgwick,* edited by Lauren Berlant, 63–71. Durham: Duke University Press, 2019.

Edwards, Jason, ed. *Bathroom Songs: Eve Kosofsky Sedgwick as a Poet.* Earth: punctum books, 2017.

———. "For Beauty Is a Series of Hypotheses? Sedgwick as Fiber Artist." In *Reading Sedgwick,* edited by Lauren Berlant, 72–91. Durham: Duke University Press, 2019.

Fawaz, Ramzi. "'An Open Mesh of Possibilities': The Necessity of Eve Sedgwick in Dark Times." In *Reading Sedgwick,* edited by Lauren Berlant, 6–33. Durham: Duke University Press, 2019.

Flatley, Jonathan. "Unlike Eve." *Criticism* 52, no. 2 (Spring 2010): 225–34. DOI: 10.1353/crt.2010.0041.

François, Anne-Lise. "Late Exercises in Minimal Affirmatives." In *Theory Aside,* edited by Jason Potts and Daniel Stout, 34–55. Durham: Duke University Press, 2014.

Gallop, Jane. "Early and Earlier Sedgwick." In *Reading Sedgwick,* edited by Lauren Berlant, 113–20. Durham: Duke University Press, 2019.

Gallop, Jane. "Sedgwick's Twisted Temporalities." In *Queer Times, Queer Becomings,* edited by E.L. McCallum and Mikko Tukhanen, 47–74. Albany: State University of New York, 2011.

Glavey, Brian. *The Wallflower Avant-Garde: Modernism, Sexuality, and Queer Ekphrasis.* Oxford: Oxford University Press, 2015.

Goldberg, Jonathan. "Eve's Future Figures." In *Reading Sedgwick*, edited by Lauren Berlant, 121-13. Durham: Duke University Press, 2019.

———. "On the Eve of the Future." *Criticism* 52, no. 2 (Spring 2010): 283-91. DOI: 10.1353/crt.2010.0040.

———. "On the Eve of the Future." *PMLA* 125, no. 2 (March 2010): 374-77. DOI: 10.1632/pmla.2010.125.2.374.

Halley, Janet. "A Tribute from Legal Studies to Eve Kosofsky Sedgwick: Introduction." *Harvard Journal of Law & Gender* 33, no. 1 (Winter 2010): 309-12. DOI: 10.2139/ssrn.3256953.

Hawkins, Katherine. "Re-Creating Eve: Sedgwick's Art and the Practice of Renewal." *Criticism* 52, no. 2 (Spring 2010): 271-82. DOI: 10.1353/crt.2010.0036.

Hawkins, Katy. "Woven Spaces: Eve Kosofsky Sedgwick's 'Dialogue on Love.'" *Women and Performance* 16, no. 2 (July 2006): 251-67. DOI: 10.1080/07407700600744568.

Herring, Scott. "Eve Sedgwick's 'Other Materials.'" *Angelaki* 23, no. 1 (February 2018): 5-18. DOI: 10.1080/0969725X.2018.1435365.

Jagose, Annamarie. "Thinkiest." *PMLA* 125, no. 2 (March 2010): 378-81. DOI: 10.1632/pmla.2010.125.2.378.

Johnson, Barbara. "Bringing Out D.A. Miller." *Narrative* 10, no. 1 (January 2002): 3-8. DOI: 10.1353/nar.2002.0002.

Lin, Lana. *Freud's Jaw and Other Lost Objects: Fractured Subjectivity in the Face of Cancer.* New York: Fordham University Press, 2017.

Miller, Nancy K. "Reviewing Eve." In *Regarding Sedgwick: Essays on Queer Culture and Critical Theory*, edited by Stephen M. Barber and David L. Clark, 217-25. New York: Routledge, 2002.

Muñoz, José Estaban. "Race, Sex, and the Incommensurate: Gary Fisher and Eve Kosofsky Sedgwick." In *Reading Sedgwick*, edited by Lauren Berlant, 152-65. Durham: Duke University Press, 2019.

Nelson, Maggie. "In the Bardo with Eve Sedgwick." *CUNY Matters* (Summer 2000): 9.

Nuland, Sherwin, B. *How We Die: Reflections on Life's Final Chapter*. New York: Vintage Books, 1995.

Proust, Marcel. *In Search of Lost Time*. 6 vols. Translated by C.K Moncrief and Terence Kilmartin. Revised by D.J. Enright. New York: Modern Library, 2003.

Rinpoche, Soygal. *The Tibetan Book of Living and Dying*. New York: HarperCollins, 2002.

Sahn, Seung. *Compass of Zen*. Edited by Hyon Gak. Boston: Shambhala Publications, 1997.

Sedgwick, Eve Kosofsky. *A Dialogue on Love*. Boston: Beacon Press, 1999.

———. "A Poem is Being Written." *Representations* 17 (Winter 1987): 110–43. DOI: 10.2307/3043795.

———. *Epistemology of the Closet*. Berkeley: University of California Press, 1990.

———. *Fat Art, Thin Art*. Durham: Duke University Press, 1994.

———, ed. *Gary in Your Pocket: Stories and Notebooks of Gary Fisher*. Durham: Duke University Press, 1996.

———. "Paranoid Reading and Reparative Reading; or, You're So Paranoid, You Probably Think This Introduction Is About You." In *Novel Gazing: Queer Readings in Fiction*, edited by Eve Kosofsky Sedgwick, 1–37. Durham: Duke University Press, 1997.

———. *Tendencies*. Durham: Duke University Press, 1993.

———. *The Weather in Proust*. Edited by Jonathan Goldberg. Durham: Duke University Press, 2011.

———. *Touching Feeling: Affect, Pedagogy, Performativity*. Durham: Duke University Press, 2003.

Sedgwick, Eve Kosofsky, and Adam Frank, eds. *Shame and Its Sisters: A Silvan Tompkins Reader*. Durham: Duke University Press, 1995.

Sedgwick, H.A. "From H.A. Sedgwick." In *Reading Sedgwick*, edited by Lauren Berlant, 34–36. Durham: Duke University Press, 2019.

Sellberg, Karin. "Queer Patience: Sedgwick's Identity Narratives." In *Reading Sedgwick,* edited by Lauren Berlant, 189–202. Durham: Duke University Press, 2019.

Soeng, Mu. *The Heart of the Universe: Exploring the Heart Sutra.* Boston: Wisdom Publications, 2010.

Solomon, Melissa. "Flaming Iguanas, Dalai Pandas, and Other Lesbian Bardos (A Few Perimeter Points)." In *Regarding Sedgwick: Essays on Queer Culture and Critical Theory,* edited by Stephen M. Barber and David L. Clark, 201–16. New York: Routledge, 2002.

Thurman, Robert A.F., trans. *The Tibetan Book of the Dead.* Composed by Padma Sambhava, discovered by Karma Lingpa. New York: Bantam Books, 1994.

Tsoukala, Philomina. "Reading 'A Poem is Being Written': A Tribute to Eve Kosofsky Sedgwick." *Harvard Journal of Law & Gender* 33, no. 1 (Winter 2010): 339–47.

Tworkov, Helen. "Obituary for Rick Fields." *Tricycle* 9, no. 1 (Fall 1999): 22–23.

Woolf, Virginia. *The Waves.* New York: Harcourt, Brace and Co., 1931.

Made in the USA
Monee, IL
17 April 2021